W9-ACG-778

The Voodoo That They Did So Well

ALSO BY STEFAN KANFER

Stardust Lost
Ball of Fire
Groucho
The Essential Groucho (editor)
Serious Business
The Last Empire
A Summer World
The International Garage Sale
Fear Itself
The Eighth Sin
A Journal of the Plague Years

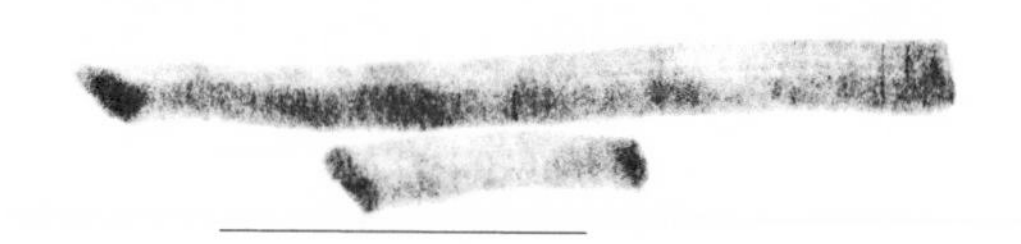

THE VOODOO THAT THEY DID SO WELL

The Wizards Who Invented the New York Stage

STEFAN KANFER

Ivan R. Dee

CHICAGO 2007

 For information, address: Ivan R. Dee, Publisher, 1332 North Halsted Street, Chicago 60622. Manufactured in the United States of America and printed on acid-free paper.

www.ivanrdee.com

Most of the contents of this book appeared originally in *City Journal*, published by the Manhattan Institute.

Library of Congress Cataloging-in-Publication Data:
Kanfer, Stefan.
The voodoo that they did so well : the wizards who invented the New York stage / Stefan Kanfer.
p. cm.
Includes bibliographical references and index.
ISBN-13: 978-1-56663-735-0 (cloth : alk. paper)
ISBN-10: 1-56663-735-x (cloth : alk. paper)
1. Theater—New York (State)—New York—History—20th century.
2. Theater—New York (State)—New York—History—19th century.
3. Theater—New York (State)—New York—Biography. I. Title.
PN2277.N5K34 2007
792.09747'1—dc22

2006032804

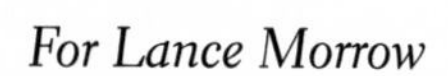

For Lance Morrow

Contents

Acknowledgments

The lives of people in show business are said to be written on wind and water. But they are also inscribed on paper, and I am particularly grateful to the biographers and historians who went before me. Some of their works are listed in a selected bibliography at the end of this book. The Library of the Performing Arts in Lincoln Center, particularly the deteriorating Billy Rose collections of newspaper clippings and photographs, remains a prime source for all who are interested in theatrical and opera history, as are relevant books and records at the Forty-second Street Library on Fifth Avenue. I have benefited enormously from their massive collections and from their patient and instructive curators. No expressions of gratitude are sufficient to recompense Myron Magnet, Brian Anderson, and my colleagues at *City Journal*, but this salute is an attempt at workmen's and workwomen's compensation. For the dozenth hardcover time I thank my encouraging and patient family, May, Lili, Andy, Lea and Aly Castle, Ethan and Daniela Kanfer. *Encore une fois.*

S. K.

Foreword

These eight pieces emerged from encouraging conversations with Myron Magnet, editor of *City Journal*, generally regarded as the nation's most influential and elegant quarterly.

Myron, a colleague from the days when we worked for *Fortune* and *Time* respectively, knew of my special interest in Manhattan's resonant past. (It had begun in childhood and continues to this day. With the exception of two years in the army and a *wanderjahr* in Europe, I have always lived in or around New York City.) He also knew of my interest in American history, literature, and entertainment, subjects I have addressed in a number of books. With his encouragement, counsel, and graceful editing, these profiles emerged. All are studies of Manhattanites past and present, men and women whose personalities are elusive but whose works are, by and large, indestructible.

Professional mourners constantly bemoan the unintelligence of the young. As a guest professor at various universities in and around the city I have not found this lament valid: the current generation of college students is as bright as my own or any other. But I *have* found a surprising incuriosity about popular history—just the sort of subject youth ought to find compelling. The reasons are manifest. The internet, video games, DVDs, iPods, and all the rest have pushed literature from center stage; the cacophony of rock, hip-hop, and grunge has obscured, and sometimes buried, some of the greatest popular melodies and lyrics ever written.

In addition, while newcomers and students appreciate contemporary Manhattan, they seem unaware of the city that used to be. In part this fault lies with the metropolis itself. The wrecking ball is so active that old neighborhoods turn into unrecognizable locales, and once-hallowed institutions become as obsolete as the corner candy store and the phone booth. Way back in 1898, John Jay Chapman noted, "The present in New York is so powerful that the past is lost." More than a hundred years later the same situation pertains—and amounts to a cultural tragedy. For the past is not only prologue, it is often an epic drama unto itself.

The story of Lorenzo Da Ponte provides a prime example. This gentleman from a Christianized Italian-Jewish family was assigned a pauper's grave within the city's precincts—an unfitting end for Mozart's greatest collaborator. The writer of *The Marriage of Figaro*, *Così Fan Tutte*, and the most sophisticated libretto of all time, *Don Giovanni*, had been a priest, a womanizer, a poet, and a professional charmer. Strapped for funds in the Old World, he sailed for America, where he sold books, ran a general store, and finally became Columbia University's first professor of Italian. (He was to be paid per pupil, but no one ever registered for his classes.) What drew him from the exalted circles of European grand opera to the shores of the New World? "A Little Touch of Mozart in New York" provides some answers and resurrects a character every bit as colorful as his Venetian friend Giacomo Casanova.

As for bygone institutions, nothing can rival vaudeville for its entertaining cast—and its unjust neglect. The old two-a-day bill has been gone since the 1950s. Even then it was only an apparition, taking ghostly curtain calls at the refurbished Palace Theater. And yet vaudeville never truly died. After it stopped supplying personalities like Mae West and Charlie Chaplin and the Marx Brothers to theater and film, it continued to influence show business. It still does. Why should old hoofers and magicians, vamps and adrenal comics be relevant in the day of cyberspace and surround sound? "Vaudeville's Brief, Shining Moment," the result of research in record collections, memoirs, and forgotten periodicals, offers some reasons.

The other entries in this book examine a range of talents and geniuses. One concerns the stars of the Yiddish theater, figures who supplied the Lower East Side with onstage excitement and offstage gossip (there was even more Dickensian melodrama in their private lives than in the ones they played before a backdrop). And five profiles address the lives and fortunes of our greatest songwriters. Irving Berlin started in abject poverty on the Bowery. Cole Porter was born into wealth; his grandfather was one of the richest men in Ohio. No matter; both men were treated as Hollywood and Broadway royalty, and both chose to make their luxurious homes in Manhattan. "I happen to like New York," wrote Porter with belligerent pride. Berlin went him one better: he bought the Music Box Theater on Forty-fifth Street.

Berlin was a happy man; he relished his long climb to the top, and he enjoyed being richer than his plutocratic father-in-law. Porter used to attend the opening nights of his shows and laugh along with the audience. Not so Richard Rodgers, a New Yorker who was raised in upper-middle-class comfort and who dressed as a businessman throughout his long career. He wrote more memorable waltzes than anyone named Strauss, and he is one of the most frequently recorded composers in the world. Wherever he went he was honored, applauded, rewarded. But these emoluments did little to assuage a lifelong depression. Rodgers's kind of suffering is hardly unknown in the annals of psychology. Many creative artists have been victims of self-doubt and melancholia; but rarely has that been the case with popular composers, who live in an atmosphere of kudos and royalty checks. The collision of celebrity and misery makes Rodgers one of the most complex figures in the Broadway pantheon.

George and Ira Gershwin brought new meaning to the word "brotherhood." Their collaboration was one of the happiest in Broadway history, broken only by George's untimely death at the age of thirty-eight. But it was also one of the most idiosyncratic. Ira was very married, self-effacing, so meticulous with rhymes that his colleagues hailed him as "The Jeweler." George was a partygoing bachelor, mercurial, ambitious, profligate with his energy and talent. He was in many senses the American Schubert, a songwriter who made his way to the classical concert hall. There is no telling how far he would have gone, but there is telling of how far he and Ira went in what historians have justly labeled the Gershwin Years.

Stephen Sondheim is scarcely less convoluted than those who preceded him. Most of his musicals venture far beyond the standard Broadway product and elevate a beleaguered, much-mocked genre. He affects to despise opera, yet the works of his middle period are in fact grand, postmodern operas every bit as demanding and melodic as Verdi's. Late Sondheim is another matter. Somewhere in the 1990s he abandoned melody, and his lyrics turned as bitter and uninviting as wormwood. It is as if there were two Sondheims, one who delighted to play with words, ideas, and tunes; the other who preferred irony to wit, and the perverse to the truly inventive. Both composers receive a thorough hearing in "Sondheim vs. Sondheim," though there is little doubt which one the biographer prefers.

In reexamining these lives and careers, I was struck once again by the city's permanently abrasive quality, its disdain for the rearview mirror, its hyperthyroid tempo—and its continual welcome to the gifted. For the young and for immigrants especially, New York was, and remains, the Promised City. When T. S. Eliot heard someone remark that old writers "are remote from us because we know so much more than they did," he replied, "Precisely, and they are that which we know." The figures in *The Voodoo That They Did So Well* not only defined themselves in the borough of Manhattan, they defined Manhattan itself. And as the following pages show, in the process they helped us, their enthusiastic audience, define ourselves.

The Voodoo That They Did So Well

A Little Touch of Mozart in New York

Amid the braying of car alarms, the thud of radio rap, the squeal and grinding of garbage trucks, New York's stony canyons and grimy streets seem a universe away from the magic and moonlight of Mozart's operas, with their harmony and balance, their moments of aching tenderness, their delicacy and subtlety, their urbane and transfiguring understanding of the human heart. But the world always turns out smaller than we think. At Calvary Cemetery in Flushing, Queens, a stone memorial facing out toward Laurel Boulevard links these Mozartean masterpieces more closely to New York than anyone sitting in Lincoln Center, swept up by the music, could possibly imagine. For the stone tells us that buried somewhere in the cemetery—where, exactly, no one knows—is the man who wrote the libretti to *The Marriage of Figaro*, *Don Giovanni*, and *Così Fan Tutte*: Lorenzo Da Ponte, New Yorker.

Unlikely, yes: but Da Ponte's whole life seems like a total fabrication. Here is a figure who rose from obscurity to create masterworks with the greatest musical mind of all time. Here is a poet who abandoned his vocation to sell tobacco. Here is a Jew who turned Catholic and worshiped at Anglican services. Here is a priest who seduced women, a teacher without pupils, a famous Italian who became an obscure American, a reverse Midas who tried to go for the gold and lost money at whatever he touched. And here too, no less improbably, is Columbia University's first professor of Italian.

According to his argumentative, self-defensive memoirs, Lorenzo Da Ponte is always correct and almost everyone else catastrophically mistaken. "I believe," he writes, "my heart is made of a different stuff than other men. I am like the soldier who, spurred on by the longing for glory, rushes against the mouth of the cannon; like the ardent lover who flings himself into the arms of a woman who torments him." Alas, "I dreamt of roses and laurels; but from the roses I had only thorns, and from the laurels bitterness! So goes the world!" An over-the-top assessment? No doubt. Then again, this was an over-the-top personality.

It is in 1783 that the name Da Ponte first crops up in the correspondence of Wolfgang Amadeus Mozart. "A certain Abbé has promised to write a new libretto," the composer informs his father. "But who knows whether he will be able to keep his word or will want to." In fact the librettist was better than his word. The first collaboration of this extraordinary pair was *The Marriage of Figaro*. How that marriage was arranged could provide the plot for a comic opera.

Lorenzo Da Ponte was born Emanuele Conegliano on March 10, 1749, in a little town near Venice. His widowed father, a Jewish leather dealer, took a second wife when the boy was fourteen. The elder Da Ponte adopted his young bride's religion, and in accordance with custom Emanuele was baptized in the name of the local bishop, Lorenzo Da Ponte. Young Lorenzo did more than genuflect to Roman Catholicism; he embraced his new faith with zeal. Quickly rising from acolyte to seminarian, he mastered Greek, Hebrew, and Latin, and became a fluent versifier in both Italian and Latin.

Church authorities recognized Lorenzo's lively intelligence, ordained him a priest, and promoted him to professor. These elevations would have sated any ordinary *arriviste*. Not Lorenzo. For him this was merely the entry to the Main Chance. For an ambitious Italian of the 1760s, Venice was the high-voltage place to be. Fashion had created a strange democracy in that city. The highly stylized masks worn in the daytime as well as at night made a newcomer always uncertain whether he was saluting a duke or a nobody. And Venice was truly an all-night town. Well past midnight, large oil lamps lit up its streets, and its bustling cafés stayed open into the small hours. Moreover, military victories, weddings, signings of treaties, religious occasions—all sparked colorful, noisy ceremonies, turning the place into an unending party. Hard for a lively young man to resist such an arena.

Without bothering to ask permission, Da Ponte took off for Venice, anxious to rub shoulders, as well as other body parts, with Europe's glitterati. Once there, the dashing young poet-priest donned his mask, wrote reams of verse, gambled, met aristocrats, and absorbed the counsel of his new friend, Giovanni Casanova. ("The easiest way to overcome a woman's virtue is to assume it is not there in the first place." "Praise the beautiful for their intelligence and the intelligent for their beauty.") He gave ear to the music that filled the public squares from dusk until dawn. It was like walking onto an opera stage. "If two of the common people walk together arm in arm," wrote a contemporary visitor, "they are always singing, and seem to converse in song; if there is company on the water, it is the same; a mere melody, unaccompanied with a second part, is not to be heard in this city; most of the ballads in the streets are to be sung to a duo."

Da Ponte's life rapidly took on aspects of a libretto. Contemporary descriptions show him as striking: elegant in stature, witty in presentation, with abundant black hair and deep-set, glowing eyes. Confuting the adage, he was lucky in cards *and* in love. His memoirs recall the day he lent a fellow gambler a handful of gold coins; in gratitude, the man offered his stepdaughter's hand in marriage. Da Ponte the man-about-town magnanimously refused; Da Ponte the memoirist neglects to mention that he had already acquired a mistress. The woman's name was Angioletta Tiepolo, and she told prying neighbors that she was Lorenzo's sister. Masked or not, the couple's deception fooled few; behind her back the neighbors whispered of "the priest's whore." Even in a place of licentiousness, the notion of a man of the cloth involved with a *demimondaine* was scandalous. For a time, Lorenzo was obliged to lie low.

What finally undid him, however, were not sexual transgressions but political ones. Among the objects Lorenzo couldn't keep sheathed was his pen. He circulated a signed poem criticizing the corrupt Venetian government. In September 1779 orders went out for the arrest of a Signor Da Ponte for the crime of sedition.

Just in time, the accused bade farewell to Venetian wagering and Venetian women and headed for the safety of the Austrian Empire. In Vienna a well-connected fellow seminarian gladly gave him a letter of introduction to a composer at the court of Emperor Joseph II. "Friend Salieri," it stated, "my good friend Da Ponte will bring you these few lines. Do for him everything that you would do for me. His heart and his talent merit whatever help you can give him."

Despite the buffeting that Antonio Salieri has received from playwright Peter Shaffer, the villain of *Amadeus* was a respected musician whose pupils included Beethoven, Schubert, and Liszt. Salieri looked over Da Ponte's portfolio of poems, measured the young man's ready wit, presentable appearance, and exquisite manners, and helped get him a job adapting the works of other writers at the Italian Theater of Vienna, the emperor's favorite cultural institution.

Before long Da Ponte was collaborating with Salieri and with a young Spanish composer, Martín y Soler. But not until Mozart entered the scene did the fledgling librettist find a creative soulmate. Never inclined to modesty, Da Ponte claimed in his memoirs: "Although Mozart was gifted with talents greater, perhaps, than those of any other composer in the world, past, present or future, he had never been able, thanks to the cabals of his enemies, to exercise his divine genius in Vienna. . . . He remained unknown and obscure, like a precious stone that, buried in the bowels of the earth, hides the brilliant prize of its splendor. I can never remember without a sense of exultation and satisfaction that Europe and the world owe in great part the exquisite vocal compositions of this wonderful genius solely to my perseverance and firmness."

Da Ponte's braggadocio was exaggerated but not false. Joseph II regarded Italian opera as superior to all others, and Mozart's rivals were quick to condemn the Salzburger *wunderkind* as incapable of writing arias, *buffa* or *seria*. Lorenzo lobbied long and hard to convince Joseph that Wolfgang Amadeus was the right man for the vocation of court composer. The emperor, who argued that Mozart wrote pieces with "too many notes," finally gave way.

Figaro was not a whimsical choice. Seeking to establish himself in Vienna with a major statement, Mozart suggested basing an opera on the Beaumarchais comedy not in spite of, but because of, its controversial plot. The play satirized the nobility and made a commoner—a haircutter, no less—the protagonist. Louis XVI had been so put off by this theme that he forbade a production on the

French stage. "We should have to destroy the Bastille," he declared, "if a performance of this play was not to be considered a dangerous blunder. This writer mocks everything that must be respected in a government."

Although he felt less insecure than Louis, the emperor was mindful of Voltaire's perception that "we live in curious times and amid astonishing contrasts: reason on the one hand, the most absurd fanaticism on the other." Joseph was torn between clinging to the ways of his forefathers and accommodating the new spirit of the age that could not long be resisted without violence. At last, in 1786, he gave permission to the musician Mozart and the poet Da Ponte—a remarkable gesture, considering that the American Revolution was less than a decade old and the French one was less than three years away. But the emperor's approach was more than amply rewarded. His country remained stable, and his place in history gains luster because he sponsored one of opera's signal achievements.

The two collaborators reinvigorated the Gallic farce about a servant, a maid, and a count. The count plots to exercise his *droit du seigneur,* the right of titled men to deflower the brides of lesser folk. The countess discovers his plan and decides to teach him, in collusion with the maid, a lesson about marriage and fidelity, a lesson that belongs not to the *ancien régime* but to the new era struggling to be born—as do the opera's attitudes about the dignity and inviolability (the *rights,* one might say) of all persons, regardless of rank. The proceedings, despite their charge of new moral and political attitudes, unfold as a wry and effervescent comedy, filled with charm and improbability—and with music whose beauty and *joie de vivre* have since made *Figaro* the world's most frequently performed opera. The debut was a sensation; audiences demanded encores from the performers—and from the authors. Da Ponte and

Mozart were only too happy to comply. Over the next three years they wrote two more operas, one dramatic, one comic, and both immortal.

Their second effort was based on Giovanni Bertati's one-act comedy about the legendary Don Juan. Without destroying the original, Da Ponte darkened it. If, under the comedy of *Figaro*, the audience can't help recalling at moments that, in real life, such a situation would have turned out much less happily, *Don Giovanni* so inextricably mixes the comic and the tragic that some singers have interpreted the Don as a frightening monster of egoistic cruelty while others have portrayed him as a much more comic embodiment of appetite and lust. As in *Figaro*, here too Da Ponte and Mozart added to their meditation on sex also a meditation on class. The collaborators' attitude is encapsulated in the Don's greeting to guests he has treated cruelly: "*Viva la libertà!*" It is a freedom he has used to take advantage of others, a freedom soon to be denied the ruling class, in events that unleashed, as it turned out, even greater abuses of freedom.

Doubtless Da Ponte had a specific voluptuary in mind: "I felt myself born for the fair sex," wrote Lorenzo's friend Casanova in his autobiography, "and I have been loved by it as often and as much as I could"—precisely the feelings of the Don, who declares, "I need women more than the bread I consume or the air I breathe." But Lorenzo must also have looked into the mirror when he considered the great roué, whose smooth approach and good looks make him a master of seduction. Many years later the librettist rationalized his numerous romances by proclaiming that he conducted only one at a time: "I have never said to a woman 'I love you' without knowing that I could love her without any breach of honor. Often my attentions, my glances and even compliments . . . were taken as declarations of love; but my mouth never sinned, and never without the consent of heart and reason did I try . . . to awaken in an innocent or credulous breast a passion which could only end in tears and remorse." The fact that Da Ponte was a serial womanizer was only one characteristic that separated him from Casanova. Unlike the elder man, the younger one had to earn a living, and he pursued his task with diligence.

Da Ponte and Mozart fashioned an opera of psychological insight and dramatic power—with that rarest attribute of opera, an alleviating sense of the absurd. Because the protagonist was no longer merely a comic object, both playwright and composer felt free to give the Don big moments and long, expressive arias that rivaled any stage drama. But whatever comedy Da Ponte took away from the Don, he gave to his sardonic servant, Leporello, who comments wryly on his master's doings and demonstrates that in art, as in life, every tragedy needs its counterweight. Da Ponte left no record of how he and Mozart collaborated. Did the tunes come first, or the lyrics? We will never know; Lorenzo was always more interested in recounting court politics than he was in describing the creative process. But a glimpse of the relationship can be found in the notes of a visitor, August Gottlieb Meissner, who was present when Mozart's friends importuned him for God's sake to finish the overture to *Don Giovanni*. With only twenty-four hours to go, the composer still had not written a note. Some sopranos enticed him indoors, then locked the room from the outside. Through a window they told him that he would be a prisoner until he produced the required pages. Mozart, Meissner recalled, "broke into laughter, despite himself, as he saw the three women singers march up in line. They had shared out the long poles from the vines, which lay in a corner of the courtyard, and to each of them had tied the various requisites that the prisoner would need for the night.

"'Here are two lamps—and a couple of bottles of wine—and cakes and sweets!' they called out as the various objects were balanced on the edge of the window-sill. Da Ponte, more down to earth than the others, appeared with a rake to which a chamber-pot was attached, and cried, 'You'll need this too. Take it, divine maestro.'

"'A pity it's empty,' Mozart retorted, 'otherwise it would be the worse for you.'

"'Good night, Mozart. Tomorrow morning early we'll come and see if the overture is ready.'

"'Yes, yes, all of us!' the ladies echoed. 'Good night, dearest Mozart, good night! Set to work.'"

The divine maestro set to work with Da Ponte one last time in 1790. Their opera *Così Fan Tutte* ("They *All* Do It") remains our culture's wisest farce. Two young bravos swear that their girlfriends love them with unshakable fidelity. Their cynical, worldly-wise older friend scoffs and proposes a bet: let them pretend to go off to war and then return, disguised as Albanian dignitaries, to attempt seductions—of *each other's* girls. Then they'll see that their inamoratas cannot remain faithful.

The men accept the wager, and the results, as all opera buffs know, are a hilarious and poignant acknowledgment of human frailty. As the canny and tolerant older friend watches the endearing Fiordiligi and Dorabella fall for two "strangers," he comments, "Everyone accuses females, but I understand if they change their affections a thousand times a day. Some call it a vice, others habit; but to me it seems a need of the heart."

Così's double understanding—that from one point of view one handsome boy is interchangeable with any other handsome boy, while from another point of view the person we choose is unique and special and the only one in the world for us—goes to the heart of the human condition, and the fondness and comic forbearance and harmony with which Mozart and Da Ponte express it is irresistible and redemptive. Da Ponte and Mozart didn't wallow in *Weltschmerz*. They knew that life was filled with tragedy, sorrow, and injustice, but it was irradiated with moments of humor, glory, hope, and love.

Through the years many critics, among them Beethoven, have taken Mozart to task for squandering his gifts on what they considered "trivia." But the trivia abides; it is the very pinnacle of man's comic genius, thanks not only to the composer's matchless music but to the librettist's sophisticated dialogue and his credible and sympathetic characters.

Alas, the magic was running out for both men. In the winter of 1790, after *Così* had been staged only five times, Emperor Joseph succumbed to a fever. The following year Mozart, overworked and impoverished, died at the age of thirty-five. In a double blow, Da Ponte had lost his noble patron and his peerless colleague. The new emperor, Leopold, smiled on new favorites.

Depressed that his standing in court had abruptly slipped, Lorenzo grew wary, then resentful. Once again he became his own worst enemy. A letter in blank verse circulated, defying the authority of the crown. Someone attributed it (correctly) to Lorenzo Da Ponte. Leopold gave Lorenzo a few months' severance pay and fired him. He decamped to Trieste, where he argued his case in letters, carried on a love affair with a leading soprano until her husband lured her back, and waited impatiently for an imperial pardon. Passing through, one of Leopold's courtiers gave him the final word: "Seek your living in Russia, in England or in France."

Da Ponte plunged into despair. But when spring came round, he met a young woman known around Trieste as *la bella inglesina*. This, it turned out, was to be the love of his life. Ann "Nancy"

Grahl was the daughter of a German merchant who had spent many years in London. (Scuttlebutt said that he, like Da Ponte, had been born Jewish; whatever the case, the Grahls now worshiped at an Anglican cathedral.) Nancy was Lorenzo's junior by twenty years. She was taken with this older man, worn smooth by experience and still a celebrity of sorts; he was beguiled by her youth and beauty. In August of that year, her father gave permission for them to wed. According to Da Ponte's lively biographer, Sheila Hodges, rumor had it—as Casanova later heard in Venice—that "Lorenzo Da Ponte threw away his priestly collar in Trieste, married a cook and fled to America."

In truth, Nancy was not a cook; she was the tutor to the children of a prosperous Dutch family. Da Ponte did not throw away his priestly collar, because he wasn't wearing one. And he and Nancy may never have exchanged official vows. His memoirs state only that they lived together "after social ceremonies and formalities." As for fleeing to the New World, that is what Nancy's parents did. Lorenzo and Nancy headed for London, where Lorenzo felt certain he could recoup his fortunes.

The sojourn was not a triumph. He wrote comic operas and—a financial catastrophe—became an impresario. He also became a publisher of libretti—his own and others'—and when that business failed, he operated a bookstore, which proved a financial disaster. He fathered two daughters. With bankruptcy looming ahead, in 1804 he encouraged his wife to take the children to the elder Grahls, now settled in Pennsylvania, while he stayed behind for one last try. In 1805, as creditors circled, he boarded a ship for Philadelphia and never saw Europe again.

John Grahl, after profitably speculating in land in rural Pennsylvania, had come to the familiar conclusion that the business of America was business. Regarding his son-in-law, he asked himself:

what would be a suitable occupation for a lyricist and playwright who had revitalized Italian opera, collaborated with Mozart, dealt with Salieri, negotiated with emperors, and jested with Casanova? Why, running a general store in the City of Brotherly Love, of course. Da Ponte drily comments on this period: "Anyone with a grain of sense can imagine how I laughed to myself every time my poetical hand weighed out two ounces of tea, or measured half a yard of plug tobacco for a cobbler or a carter, or a morning dram costing three cents."

Lorenzo was now in his late fifties and the father of two girls and three boys, the eldest thirteen, the youngest in swaddling clothes. Grimly acknowledging that buying and selling might not be his forte, he relocated to New York City. Here he planned to become an Italian and Latin tutor. That was not to be. New Yorkers held the Da Pontes at arm's length. Lorenzo feared he'd have to throw himself on the mercy of Nancy's father, who had made no secret of his doubts about his son-in-law's competence.

But fortunately, one day in 1809, Da Ponte dropped into Riley's bookstore on lower Broadway and happened to overhear the proprietor discussing European culture with a learned young gentleman. They were speaking of Metastasio, and Lorenzo dared to interrupt. "I knew the poet personally," he declared. "And as for Mozart. . . ." He went on dropping names and telling stories. His mesmerized listeners begged him to go on.

The young gentleman introduced himself. He was Clement Moore, who would one day enter history (perhaps spuriously, a recent scholar contends) as the author of "The Night Before Christmas." Clement had distinguished himself by becoming, at nineteen, the valedictorian of his class at Columbia College—the college presided over by his father, Bishop Benjamin Moore. At the moment he was a dilettante, scholar, and occasional versifier on such subjects as yellow fever and the hazards of alcohol. Unlike most prosperous New York burghers, Clement had no bias against newcomers to the city, respected the work of foreign writers, and couldn't wait to introduce Lorenzo to his friends.

The Da Pontes became the catch of the social season. At the Moores' house they mixed with distinguished company, chatting of the Old World and the New. Nancy charmed the company by speaking English without an accent. Lorenzo, Mozart's co-worker—Wolfgang Amadeus Mozart!—went on about the extravagances of Dante, the conceits of Petrarch, the plagiarisms of Boccaccio. He quoted the Bible in Hebrew and Latin; he quoted Virgil, Horace, Dante. His eyes still glowed, his bearing was elegant, aided by the cane he carried as a swagger stick. His courtly mien and soft, sibilant accent were as irresistible here as in Europe—except that in America he used them to win friends rather than to charm females.

The trouble was that this enchanting couple was stony broke. Something, the guests decided, simply had to be done. And so it was. With their encouragement and a little financial assistance, Lorenzo opened the Manhattan Academy for Young Gentlemen, and, as it would not do for males and females to mix in the classroom, Nancy founded the Manhattan Academy for Young Ladies. With a position and an income, Da Ponte regained his footing. He not only taught class but also began to import and sell Italian books. He built a small theater and staged Italian plays. He wrote poems, including one urging his fellow Americans to support England in its fight against Napoleon—the enemy, it goes without saying, of his native country.

But after several years of this, Lorenzo began to feel caged and restless. The tyros in the classroom were too raw, too . . . American. They knew nothing of opera and next to nothing of Mozart, the Italian court, poetry, the classic tongues. And they must have found their teacher too sophisticated, too full of recondite allusions for them to follow. Lorenzo abandoned the classroom and the city for a big spread in Sunbury, Pennsylvania, not far from John Grahl's dwelling place. There he could get away from the glazed stare of students and relax amid quarries and waterfalls, deer and pheasant. To fill up the days, he palavered with neighbors and sold liquor and medical supplies.

But this too failed to satisfy. The woods would always be foreign turf to an *homme du monde*, and when New York beckoned two years later, Lorenzo changed his mind and locale yet again. This time he responded to an invitation from the ever-patient Clement Moore, who promised that he would recruit bright, interested pupils to sit at Da Ponte's feet and learn of Italy's great literature.

The seventy-five-year-old Da Ponte was to roam no more. He became Manhattan's ambassador without portfolio for Italian culture, pointing out that in practically every city in the United States "one finds the wines and grapes of Sicily, the oil, the olives, and the silk of Florence, the marble of Carrara, the gold chains of Venice, the cheese of Parma, the sausages of Bologna, and even the macaroni of Naples and the plaster figurettes of Lucca. Yet, to the shame of our country, there is not, in the whole of America, a bookstore kept by an Italian! All the books in this city, aside from the volumes I introduced myself, have either been brought casually by travelers, or have been sold at auction with other books on the death of some foreign inhabitant." The indefatigable booster established an Italian library within the New York Public Library (where the six hundred volumes still reside).

In 1825, Clement Moore persuaded his father, the bishop, to make room for the seventy-six-year-old Signor Da Ponte as Columbia's first professor of Italian. Lorenzo would be paid according to the number of pupils who took his course. In the first year, twenty-eight students turned up. For the next thirteen years, not a single freshman, sophomore, junior, or senior registered for Italian at Columbia. The philosophical Da Ponte took to referring to himself as *Professor Sine Exemplo*, meaning both an unprecedented professor and a peerless professor—a pun that contrasts in typical Da Ponte fashion his lack of success with his incomparable merit.

As such, he carried on outside the university, lecturing on Dante, composing more verse, translating Italian writers. The Da Pontes had become a shabby genteel pair, guests rather than hosts, with the seventy-something Lorenzo still attempting to play the star at parties, *Sunset Boulevard*–style ("I *am* big; it's the operas that got small"). To define his importance, Da Ponte began to issue his memoirs in installments. These gave him a chance to trail names, review an adventurous life, and get in a few cracks about the ignorant press. "This one writes a three-page article in praise of the wrinkled throat of a eunuch; that one announces the arrival of an elephant and two monkeys in such-and-such a town; and a hundred similar things of no account; and in more than 20 years not one charitable writer has been found who has deigned to put down in black on a small piece of paper, so that the literary world, and in particular the Italians, may learn about it, what I have done in America!"

In 1831 his beloved Nancy suddenly died of pneumonia, and Lorenzo sensed the chill of mortality in his own bones. There was still much to do. He borrowed funds in order to bring over a company of Italian singers. They performed many arias, including two by a relative newcomer, Gioachino Rossini. But with no head for business, Da Ponte, as before, lost money, even though he hawked libretti in the lobby himself. Undeterred, he raised more funds from New York philanthropists, including former mayor Philip Hone, and oversaw the building of the city's first Italian opera house, a Greek Revival building on the Bowery. It was, Hone later noted in his diary, "the neatest and most beautiful theater in the United States and unsurpassed in Europe," with its boxes hung with crimson silk, its emblematic medallions and octagonal panels of crimson, blue, and gold, and its dome embellished with paintings of the Muses.

The opera house opened in the fall of 1833 to universal acclaim. A contemporary ticket holder recalled Da Ponte's "tall figure and handsome face at the opera . . . infecting others with his enthusiasm, and serving as a vital bond between the musical strangers and the fascinated public." That public had a short attention span, though, and over the next several years Da Ponte personally lost four thousand dollars. His investors went in the hole for much more. (Despite an attempt to depose Boston as America's cultural center, New York City was still a provincial arena, unready for Mozart or Gluck; the first profitable opera house was not to rise on Astor Place for another twenty-five years.) The management changed hands, the Italian Opera House became the National Theater, a venue for legitimate productions, and three years later it burned to the ground. Given these circumstances, Lorenzo's rhyming reproach to his Yankee public, if ungracious, is surely understandable:

Yet to the hand which has those treasures given
Ye have refused the cimbal and the lyre;
And from this brow the laurel crown have riven
Whose name has set the proudest stage afire!

He pushed on, regardless. Now that Nancy was gone, the old man, *sans* teeth but with an abundance of grey hair and undiminished energy, invited young intellectuals to his run-down home to debate the virtues of the New World and the Old. One of his guests left an impression of those encounters: "It was my pleasure to dine at Da Ponte's place and hear furious discussions of Italian politics and delectable praise of composers and vocalists or pictorial critiques—transported by magic from Broome Street to the Piazza Vecchia or the Via Condotta. . . . Corned beef versus macaroni, was the problem he loved to state and to solve."

Still arguing and advocating, still trying to fuse culture and commerce, Da Ponte died of consumption in 1838 at eighty-nine, an extraordinary age in the early nineteenth century. Those who had shortchanged or betrayed him were no longer on the scene in Europe or America—every man jack of them had passed on, he was pleased to note. All the same, Lorenzo could not claim to be truly fulfilled. Toward the close of his life he wrote: "If, when I was young, I had read the story of a man to whom the things had happened which have happened to me, and whose conduct was more or less similar to mine, how many mistakes I should have been able to avoid, the consequences of which have cost me so many tears and are still afflicting me so greatly in my old age! Thus I can and must say with Petrarch, 'I know my faults and do not excuse them,' but the damage, at my age, cannot be remedied, and all that remains to me is repentance."

What are we to make of Da Ponte's fate? Did he deserve obscurity? Didn't the librettist merely ride a whirlwind? Couldn't Mozart set Euclid's *Elements of Geometry* to music and magically turned the mathematician into a profound and lyrical poet? Almost two centuries later, Lorenzo's defenders could provide a definitive answer, when Igor Stravinsky pronounced himself pleased with the libretto for *The Rake's Progress* provided by W. H. Auden and Chester Kallman. It was, the composer said, the finest since those three works Da Ponte had written with Mozart. Maestro Stravinsky understood that the first-rate librettist must write characters and think music, a profoundly difficult task that Da Ponte did peerlessly.

Let his ghost take note: at last one charitable writer has deigned to put down in black on a small piece of paper what Da Ponte did in America, as well as in Venice and Vienna—and to celebrate the achievement. Bravo, Lorenzo, bravissimo!

Vaudeville's Brief, Shining Moment

It was the most democratic popular art in American history. To get onstage, all you needed was chutzpah and moxie. If you had the right stuff, you picked up the dance steps, the vocal style, the comic timing that could make you a star—maybe even one of the Marx Brothers. No wonder their mother, Minnie, loved vaudeville. "Where else," she asked, "could you go so far without knowing anything?" And millions of fans and thousands of performers agreed. Yet despite its profound influence on every facet of entertainment, from the musical to the television sitcom, American vaudeville had a trajectory as astonishingly brief—if sparkling—as a Roman candle.

The word "vaudeville" derives from the French *vau-de-vire*, referring to the Valley of the Vire in Normandy, where itinerant singers amused the crowds with double entendre–packed songs. The tradition soon crossed the pond and by the mid-nineteenth century had become even trashier. Coarse buffoons and loose women formed the customary fare. In *Huckleberry Finn* those two wandering frauds, the King and the Duke, offer a typical act, the

Royal Nonesuch. In big type the handbill warns customers: women and children not admitted. "There," says the Duke, admiring his handiwork. "If that line don't fetch them, I don't know Arkansaw!" The routine, Huck reports, features the King "a-prancing out on all fours, naked; and he was painted all over, ring-streaked-and-striped, all sorts of colors, as splendid as a rainbow. . . . Well, it would have made a cow laugh to see the shines that old idiot cut."

Such travesties placed vaudeville performers at the bottom tier of show business, at a time when even legitimate theater folk drew suspicion. "Respectable" hotels and restaurants barred vaudevillians. The rooming houses and cafeterias that did admit them were always on the wrong side of the tracks. Even in more relaxed New York City, reformers began closing in during the last two decades of the nineteenth century.

And then came an unexpected moral turnaround, as profound as the change in Victorian society from loose to upright. The King-and-Duke sort of vaudeville received the thorough laundering it needed in 1881, when Tony Pastor, owner of a Fourteenth Street New York music hall, made the calculation that Walt Disney repeated some fifty years later: a theater that excluded women and children curtailed its income by at least 67 percent.

The plump, mustachioed impresario had been showing pirated and racy versions of Gilbert and Sullivan, among them *The Pie Rats of Pen Yan*. Now Pastor shut his adjoining barroom, forbade smoking (he was always ahead of his time), and presented a carefully supervised variety program. All performers had to clean up their acts before they dared step upon his stage. Obscenity, vulgarity, and irreverence became taboo. Gone were such saline japes as:

MAN: My sister-in-law thinks "lettuce" is a proposition.
WOMAN: She never married, did she?
MAN: No, her children wouldn't let her.

And:

> WOMAN: Someone is fooling with my knee.
> MAN: It's me, and I'm not fooling.

Nor could patrons hear the closing song made famous in British music halls and sung on the streets of America:

> What's that for, eh? Oh, tell me Ma.
> If you won't tell me, I'll ask Pa.
> But Ma said, "Oh, it's nothing,
> Hold your row."
> Well, I've asked Johnny Jones, see,
> So I know now!
> (CURTAIN)

Those who ignored the new rules wound up in burlesque, defined by a contemporary edition of *Webster*'s as: "A theatrical entertainment of broad and earthy humor; consists of comic skits and short turns (and sometimes striptease)." The same dictionary described vaudeville more approvingly: "A stage entertainment of successive separate performances, usually songs, dances, acrobatic acts, dramatic sketches."

Thus arrived the first family shows, where wives, husbands, kids, even unescorted women could while away an evening without blushing. The new conventions and standards weren't easy for performers to meet, however. As Charles and Louise Samuels observe in *Once Upon a Stage*, the majority of vaudevillians emerged from the slums, uneducated and untrained. After winning an amateur night or two, a performer would usually find himself booked into a small theater in a backwater—and often in a state—where he had never been before. Vaudevillians had to "discover by themselves how to dress, walk on the stage, talk to the audience with just the right mixture of humility and pride, find the right songs and material." In addition to the intimidating audience that lyricist Oscar Hammerstein II called the "Big Black Giant," "there were bad-tempered, dictatorial house managers who took delight in cutting your material, hounding you, doing everything possible to break your spirit."

Performers with bulletproof egos kept going; the others faded away. It was a hard life. Of some twenty thousand choristers, group acts, and soloists performing across America, fewer than 2 percent would make a good living in vaudeville. Fewer still would enjoy celebrity. Yet *Times* critic Brooks Atkinson was right: despite its drawbacks, vaudeville gave audiences "a brilliant form of stage entertainment that expressed skill, personality and ideas, and presented some of the most talented actors of all time."

Those talents have long since vanished, and so have the venues where they performed, razed or transformed into octoplex movie houses. Vanished too are producers with the audacity and instinct that breathed life into vaudeville—producers like Oscar Hammerstein I, grandfather of the lyricist. The German immigrant began his career as a cigar maker, developed a machine for turning out stogies with compressed air, obtained patents for several other inventions, and invested the income in real estate. He put up a couple of theaters in Harlem, parlayed the profits into an opera house on Thirty-fourth Street and Broadway, and then made the move that would win him the title "The Creator of Times Square."

Between Forty-fourth and Forty-fifth Streets on Broadway, then a nondescript part of midtown, Oscar erected the Olympia, encompassing a music hall, a theater, and a smaller concert arena. To control every aspect of show business, he hired his three sons as supervisors. Harry looked after construction, Arthur took care of the decorating, and Willie (father of Oscar II) booked the talent that would appear at the posh new houses.

Trouble is, the houses were costly and wasteful as well as grand. Even after selling off his other properties, Oscar had to declare bankruptcy in 1898. Broke, he ran into a friend. "My fortune," he sighed, "consists of two cigars. I will share it with you." In fact, no one could take his greatest assets from him—his self-confidence and his gift for self-promotion. He talked friends into lending him some venture capital and built yet another theater, the Victoria, located between Forty-second and Forty-third Streets on Broadway. A reporter described it as "a big, tinkling pearl box—all white and gold with the opals of electricity studding it in profusion, gorgeous carpets, splendid lounges, and all the ultra-elegance of an ultra-elegance-loving metropolis."

Hammerstein began with dramas and musical shows before turning the Victoria into a two-a-day vaudeville house. Thoroughly modern Willie booked popular singers and comedians, and a very different sort of headliner—the kind who made the front and back pages of the tabloids: Jack Johnson, the first black heavyweight champ; Lady Hope, who showed off the enormous Hope diamond; and Captain Cook, who claimed (falsely) to have discovered the North Pole.

Other producers, taking note, began to flourish their own celebrities: the brilliant blind and deaf Helen Keller, who did nothing but answer a few questions written into her palm; the saloon-smashing prohibitionist Carrie Nation; and the silent but scandalous "girl on the red velvet swing," Evelyn Nesbitt, whose husband, drug-addicted socialite Harry K. Thaw, had murdered her former lover, the world-renowned architect Stanford White (audiences happily paid good money for a glimpse of the first twentieth-century sex kitten).

On occasion, Willie erred. The heavyweight champion John L. Sullivan starred in a truncated *Uncle Tom's Cabin* and noticed that the actor playing Uncle Tom was getting more applause. The Great John L. erupted one night after "Tom" took his fifth bow, and chased him into the street. But Willie rarely went wrong when he took the murderess route. Florence Burns had shot her lover in Brooklyn after he had dumped her for another woman. Let off on probation, she used the time to play in vaudeville. At the Victoria, Florence tried a dance step or two to show that she could do something with her feet as well as her hands, but the routine failed to please the critics. One compared her to "a sidewheel steamer catching a porpoise." The crowds came to gawk anyway. Other glamorous criminals included Ethel Conrad and Lillian Graham, who had conspired to kill W. E. D. Stokes, a rich hotel owner. Willie billed them "The Shooting Stars."

Effective as the Hammersteins could be at vaudeville presentations, their efforts paled beside those of two shrewd New England impresarios, Benjamin Franklin Keith and Edward Franklin Albee. Keith began his ascent in the circus, running a sideshow populated with freaks, strongmen, fortune-tellers, and other wonders. He hired Albee (adoptive grandfather of the playwright) to look after the animals. E. F. was just as smart as B. F., and soon the men worked as equals, operating the Keith Circuit, a string of vaudeville houses across the country.

Keith was an upright, hands-on manager who repaired the broken seats himself. His parsimonious, deeply religious wife scrubbed the floors of the theaters near their Manhattan office and ran a boardinghouse for actors. She made certain that no ladies showed up in single gentlemen's rooms after dark. And she saw to it that the artistes' onstage behavior never embarrassed the Keith name. A young juggler, Fred Allen, who later put down his Indian clubs and became a radio superstar, recalled a sign posted backstage along the Keith-Albee circuit:

NOTICE TO PERFORMERS
Don't say "slob" or "son-of-a-gun" or "hully gee" on this stage unless you want to be canceled peremptorily. Do not address anyone in the audience in any manner. If you have not the ability to entertain Mr. Keith's audiences without risk of offending them, do the best you can. Lack of talent will be less open to censure than would be an insult to a patron. If you are in doubt as to the character of your act, consult the local manager before you go on the stage, for if you are guilty of uttering anything sacrilegious or even suggestive, you will be immediately closed and will never again be allowed in a theater where Mr. Keith is in authority.

Albee was no less rigid, but profit, not deportment, consumed him. In 1902, when a group of actors decided to unionize, he bought off the leaders with two-year contracts, shattering the organization. Six years later, when S. Z. Poli, owner of a smaller string of New England theaters, decided to break the Keith-Albee stranglehold by booking talent on his own, Albee promptly informed banks in every city with a Poli theater that the Keith circuit planned to build a grand theater there, which would doubtless drive the town's other vaudeville houses out of business. When the banks called in all of Poli's outstanding debts, he agreed to book his performers through the Keith office.

The following year the Keith houses raked in some $30 million. As Albee had made his point fiscally, Keith had made his morally. Under his aegis, vaudeville not only acquired class; it became as formalized as a minuet. In his online history of vaudeville, John Kenrick describes the typical bill of fare at major houses. "The 'Opening' was a 'silent act' that would not be ruined by the bustle of an audience settling in"—trained seals and acrobats, say. Next came juvenile acts like the Gumm Sisters, whose youngest member later changed her name to Judy Garland, and the Nicholas Brothers, dancing troupers who subsequently became headliners. A comedy sketch or one-act play would follow. Customarily these featured names from the legitimate theater, including Sarah Bernhardt, Alfred Lunt, and the Barrymores—Lionel, John, and Ethel.

Then came an eccentric novelty act. This might involve a magician who sawed his spangled assistant in half, or a mind reader, or a trio like the Three Keatons: mother, father, and Buster, "the Human Broom"—father Keaton delighted audiences by grabbing his son by the ankles and sweeping tables, chairs, and the floor with the boy's hair. Other favorites included the escape artist Houdini, who would emerge from a sealed coffin; Julian Eltinge, a female impersonator; and Julius Tannen, a monologist celebrated for his word pictures: he said that using a paper cup reminded him of drinking out of a letter, and excused himself for being late by explaining that he had squeezed out too much toothpaste and couldn't get it back into the tube. A little girl caught his act in upstate New York; to her, Tannen was pure enchantment: "Just this voice," wrote Lucille Ball, "and this magnificent man enthralling you with his stories, his intonations. He changed my life. I knew it was a very serious, wonderful thing to be able to make people laugh and/or cry, to be able to play on their emotions."

Celebrities of note, famous or notorious, held fifth place. That brought down the curtain on Part One.

Part Two opened with a large set and a lot of people onstage. Choirs, novelty orchestras, and trained tiger-and-lion acts were favorites.

The seventh spot—"next to closing" in vaudeville-speak—was for the big names. One of the customers' favorite teams, Ed Gallagher and Al Shean (the Marx Brothers' uncle), spouted doggerel inspired by the headlines or by old jokes set to rhyme and music.

> SHEAN: Oh, Mr. Gallagher, oh, Mr. Gallagher.
> GALLAGHER: Hello, what's on your mind this morning, Mr. Shean?
> SHEAN: Everybody's making fun
> Of the way our country's run,
> All the papers say
> We'll soon live European.
> GALLAGHER: Why, Mr. Shean, why Mr. Shean,
> On the day they took away our old canteen,
> Cost of living went so high
> That it's cheaper now to die.
> SHEAN: Positively, Mr. Gallagher.
> GALLAGHER: Absolutely, Mr. Shean.
> (CURTAIN)

Those gentlemen enjoyed a comparatively brief, if intense, vogue and never crossed over to the new media of film and radio. Other headliners did, including Keaton, Jack Benny, W. C. Fields, Al Jolson, Sophie Tucker, the Marx Brothers, Charlie Chaplin (whom Fields grumpily described as "a God-damned ballet dancer"), George Burns and Gracie Allen, and Eddie Cantor.

The finale was for acts on the way down. By now patrons were donning coats, chatting, and heading for the aisles. If they bothered to turn around, they saw a monotonous singer, a cacophonous one-man band, a juggler of little note. Occasionally these bookings surprised. The Cherry Sisters were so inept that they won a pre-camp eminence. Ranging in number from two to five, the group sang off-key and had such bad timing that audiences threw vegetables at them: an enterprising manager began to sell produce outside the theater. The Cherries warbled behind a net to avoid injury.

In the new century these performances that cost so little—rarely more than a dollar—and gave so much, beguiled not just the common folk but intellectuals too. As novelist William Dean Howells wrote in *Harper's*, "I am an inveterate vaudeville-goer, for the simple reason that I find better acting, and better drama, than you get on your legitimate stage."

Moving up the vaudeville ladder could be as hard as a shortstop's climb from Class B to the majors. Nostalgia sweetens entertainers' recollections; their memoirs often throw a golden light on the early years of mean boardinghouses, meager salaries, and hecklers. Still, the best of them are candid about the long and arduous climb to the top of the marquee.

Brooklyn-born Mae West put in years as a shrewd, ambitious chorine before scoring with a series of risqué Hollywood films that resuscitated nearly bankrupt Paramount Pictures in the 1930s. She never failed to praise vaudeville as the night school where she learned "to adjust mood, tempo and material." The husky-voiced high-camp temptress went on to observe, archly, "I didn't get it from books."

Neither did Minnie Marx's son Arthur, better known as Harpo. "If an audience didn't like the Marx Brothers," he wrote, "we had no trouble finding it out." Southern audiences pelted the Yorkville kids "with sticks, bricks, spitballs, cigar butts, peach pits and chewed-out stalks of sugarcane. We took all this without flinching—until Minnie gave us the high sign that she'd collected our share of the receipts. Then we started throwing the stuff back at the audience and ran like hell for the railroad station the second the curtain came down."

Arthur's studious brother Julius remembered Mama pushing him onstage in tank town after tank town, then city after city, watching the young man invent and reinvent himself with an accumulation of staccato delivery, insult jokes, outrageous puns, and fluid slouch. "When we were playing small-time vaudeville," he told a friend years later, "I would try a line and if it got a laugh, I'd leave it in. If it didn't get a laugh, I'd take it out and write another line. Pretty soon, I had a character called Groucho."

A rotund young woman made her entry one amateur night in Connecticut—and got the hook even before she stepped onstage. "This one's so ugly," said the theater manager, "the crowd up front will razz her. Better get some cork and black her up. She'll kill 'em." That she did, and Sophie Tucker, the Last of the Red Hot Mamas, remained in blackface, hiding her race, if not her talent, for five years.

Fred Astaire (né Austerlitz) from Omaha also harkened back to his days as a vaudeville hoofer. He and sister Adele opened a show in New York—and met with silence. The next day they cased the board listing the order of acts. A "cold sweat set in when I couldn't find our names anywhere at all," Astaire wrote.

"Confused, I went to the doorman and asked him what this meant.

"'Sonny,' he said, 'I heard the manager say they had to make a change. Why don't you run out to his office and see him? He's there now.'

"We went out and got the story from the manager. He said simply, 'I'm sorry kids—your act wasn't strong enough. You've been canceled.' That was it. There is no worse blow to a vaudevillian than that word 'canceled.'" The Astaires persevered nonetheless. Adele married a British aristocrat and retired from the stage. And Fred . . . well.

Bob Hope had trouble getting started too. He ruefully recollected a time in Texas: "When I walked before my first Fort Worth audience with my fast talk, I might as well have kept walking to the

Rio Grande. Nobody cared. I couldn't understand it. I came back offstage, threw my derby on the floor and told the unit manager, 'Get me a ticket back to my own country.'"

George Burns, who eventually joined with his wife Gracie to become one of the prime comedians of radio and television and film, had a similarly rough beginning. Week after week he would change his name, hoping that a fresh reputation would rise from the ashes of the previous one. "I joined up with another guy, and we called the act Burns and Links. My name was Links. Confusing isn't it? We were a two-man dancing act, and couldn't get a job anywhere." Sitting outside an agent's office, they overheard him speaking on the phone: "I could use a dog act in Ronkonkoma." George asked the receptionist to give her boss a message. "Burns and Links and their dogs are sitting outside." Landing a one-night contract for ten dollars, the pair quickly acquired two stray mutts. "The act opened with eight bars of an introduction, 'Down Among the Sheltering Pines,' pianissimo, offstage, then a repeat of eight bars same, forte, and we would run onstage holding our straw hats high in the air with one hand so the audience could see the red linings. This time we ran out, hats in the air, and dogs under our arms. We dropped the dogs, finished the act, collected the $10, and I changed my name again." When it became Burns, and he got a partner named Allen, it was gravy from then on.

William Claude Dukenfield, better known as W. C. Fields, switched from juggler to comedian in his vaudeville years. He described the metamorphosis, starting with "a trick in which I toss a silk hat on the rim of which lies a lighted cigar, from my foot, balancing a hat on my nose as it falls, while I catch the cigar and go on smoking. Half the time I fail to do it on the first trial, but by means of a lot of little extra comedy turns following the failure, I usually succeed in making my audience believe my failure is intentional. Though my regular time is 21 minutes, I rarely get through in less than 25 or 26 minutes. The additional time is taken up with laughter."

Fields's contemporary, another New Yorker named Milton Berle (né Berlinger), had his own vaudeville memories. "It took monologists like Jack Benny and Bob Hope and me 18 months to two years to get seven solid minutes to put into an act," Berle observed. "You weeded out the crap, deleted and edited stuff that wouldn't play. Then when you went to Wilkes-Barre, it had to be changed again. And then another town, and still more changes." Shaking his head, he asked rhetorically, "Where can you get that kind of training today?"

Every one of these headliners began in "Small Time"—little theaters where they made maybe fifteen dollars a week while they polished their dance steps and songs or tried out new jokes. One manager "who was in the raincoat business," Fred Allen recalled, "tried to talk the actors into taking their salaries in raincoats." In Bayonne, New Jersey, Allen went on, "during my act, a cat came down the aisle, emitted a series of blood-curdling cries, and delivered a litter on the carpet." Riposted Allen, "I thought my act was a monologue, not a catalogue."

The most promising troupers moved on to "Medium Time"—second-class theaters in first-class cities, at salaries from seventy-five to a few hundred dollars a week. In one of those houses a New York hoofer named James Cagney broke into show business. "A three-act," he recalled, "needed a replacement for one of their number. This act was Parker, Rand and Leach, and Mr. Leach was Archie Leach, now known to history as Cary Grant." In Medium Time, Cagney found that vaudevillians "knew something that ultimately I came to understand and believe—that audiences are the ones who determine material. I remember Dr. Johnson's couplet: 'The drama's laws, the drama's patrons give, / And we who live to please must please to live.'"

"Big Time" was the acme—a two-a-day format in the top venues in major cities. Those in the "next to closing" slot earned well over a thousand dollars a week, when the average workman took home forty dollars for five and a half days' labor. Fields belonged in that august company; so did comedienne Fanny Brice, the kilted Scotsman Sir Harry Lauder, Bob Hope, Jack Benny, Fred Allen, and the former Metropolitan Opera singer Fritzi Sheff. An awed Buster Keaton recalled the week that he played on a bill with her: "This little lady carried 36 pieces of luggage and an entourage consisting of her pianist, a chauffeur, a footman and two French maids." A week before she arrived in each city, Keaton reports, she'd send an interior decorator to redo her suite and dressing room, with "magnificent mirrors with gold frames and drapes suitable to one of the fabulous boudoirs at Versailles."

Big Time's center was New York City. After Hammerstein, Albee, and Keith, producer Martin Beck, who had recently bombed in Chicago, tried again on the Great White Way in 1913, with a brand-new Palace Theater in the theater district's heart. But as the last coats of paint went on and the last members of the cast signed short-term contracts, the Hammersteins announced that Beck had violated an agreement. Their Victoria Theater owned exclusive rights to all Keith vaudeville acts from Thirty-fourth Street to Columbus Circle. With a large, glistening theater and no one to play in it, Beck agreed to buy the Hammersteins' rights to the talent for an unheard-of $225,000. On opening night, critics lauded the 1,800 plush seats, huge crystal chandeliers, ivory and bronze decorations, and lobby walls of Siena marble—but not the headline act: La Napierowska, a Polish danseuse.

The *World* scoffed at the "Polish representative of the great horde of wriggle dancers who have swooped down on New York. This lady was supposed to be stung by a bee. She divested herself of her clothing to find it. She called herself a classical dancer but no one seemed to notice it." The comedian at the bottom of the bill was swept away with the debris, and Ed Wynn, like the danseuse, pushed on. Willie Hammerstein gloated over the Palace's dim future: "I give it six months."

His crystal ball was cloudy. As the theater entered its sixth week of half-life, Beck engaged established superstar Ethel Barrymore. She appeared in a one-act melodrama by dashing journalist Richard Harding Davis, who had covered the Spanish-American and Boer wars. The bill also boasted the singing Courtney Sisters; Bessie Clayton, a brilliant ballet dancer; and Nat Wills, "The Comedy Tramp." Wills's wife had been a circus bareback rider; when they split, he laconically drawled: "I should have married the horse." They all played to SRO houses.

Following that bill came Sarah Bernhardt, the French stage doyenne. Emoting in English, she treated onlookers to the death scene from *Camille* and surefire excerpts from other European dramas. Every performance of her seventeen-day run overflowed. *Variety* had ridiculed the Palace's "outrageous" policy of charging $2 for the best seats; now the theater asked $2.50, and scalpers got as much as $10 for a pair.

After that the Palace was a symbol of accomplishment. If an act could make it there, it could make it anywhere. Entertainers who had appeared at that theater never let anyone forget it. One manager of another theater wearily nailed a sign near his dressing rooms:

DON'T TELL ME HOW YOU KILLED THEM AT THE PALACE
DO IT HERE

Yet with all the power that vaudeville exerted, it still lacked a final ingredient: elegance. That was B.Z.: Before Ziegfeld. Like Martin Beck, Florenz Ziegfeld had started off in Chicago, where his father owned a failing nightclub. As a last resort he let young Flo take over the bookings. In came "The World's Strongest Man," a mesomorph named George Sandow, who wrestled a drugged lion and turned the season into a winner. Next stop: Broadway. After producing a few so-so musicals, Ziegfeld had a brief marriage to singer Anna Held. She left Flo with bitter memories and one thing of value: the suggestion to stage a revue patterned after the Folies Bergère of Paris.

The Ziegfeld Follies debuted in 1907 at the New York Theater's roof garden, where evening breezes eased the fierce summer heat. From the start, the impresario sought the best talent in show business. His director was Julian Mitchell, a former dancer who would put his head against a piano to feel a song's beat, and then create dynamic staging for it. Designing the scenery was the great art-deco architect Joseph Urban. Lady Duff-Gordon and Erté did the costumes. Follies comedians included Bert Williams, the first black luminary to star on the same stage with white folks; lariat-twirling Will Rogers; Eddie Cantor; the original Funny Girl, Fanny Brice; the dancing Dolly Twins, who would mirror each other's moves perfectly; and Ed Wynn, the bottom-of-the-bill comic Flo had spotted at the Palace during its disastrous opening weeks. Even with all this talent, the key ingredient was the line of females singing the songs and wearing the skimpy (though always decorous) fur-trimmed or spangled costumes. Irving Berlin's song, written at Ziegfeld's behest, said it all:

A pretty girl is like a melody
That haunts you night and day.

Just like the strain
Of a haunting refrain,
She'll start upon
A *marathon*
And run around your brain.

Berlin's number became the *Follies'* unofficial anthem, but Ziegfeld showcased a series of best-selling tunes, including "Shine On Harvest Moon," "By the Light of the Silvery Moon," and "Second Hand Rose," the comic number that made Fannie Brice's reputation—and Barbra Streisand's two generations later.

When the United States entered the Great War, Ziegfeld, now married to the beautiful actress Billie Burke, decked his chorines out in military uniforms—except for one who bared a breast, impersonating Liberty as shown in various paintings. In the midst of this triumph came the horrific 1918 flu epidemic, in which some 550,000 Americans died in a matter of weeks, forcing theaters to close around the country. It nearly ruined Flo. But he hung on out of a stubborn belief in himself and in the future, presenting show after show to almost empty houses as he edged closer to insolvency. His faith held. The plague stopped as suddenly as it had begun, and customers trickled back. The boom picked up where it had left off, and by the end of the War to End All Wars, as historian John Kenrick notes, "a subtle yet momentous change had taken place. America had shifted from being a debtor nation to being a lender to the world." The citizens wanted to party, and vaudeville led the way.

The party briefly broke up in 1919, after the nascent Actors Equity Association, demanding better pay and job security, struck, and the Stagehands Union honored the walkout. Almost every theater shut down. The producers recognized Equity and met its demands, and reopened their shows, gratified to see that the lines of ticket buyers reached clear around the block. Equity didn't represent black performers, however. Instead the Theater Owners Booking Agency—TOBA—represented "colored" performers, who played to all-Negro audiences in segregated theaters. The actors said the initials really stood for Tough On Black Asses, because the fees fell far below those paid up north. These stars developed a hard glitter: Ma Rainey and Bessie Smith became recording stars; Bill "Bojangles" Robinson went on to Broadway and Hollywood.

By now Ziegfeld's success had encouraged others to cash in on the postwar festivities. The Shuberts, theater owners and producers, offered a series of revues called *Artists and Models*. George White, a dancer turned impresario, labeled his shows *The Scandals*. While Flo was still covering the American Girl, White, sensing a Roaring Twenties swing away from propriety, was busy undressing her. *The Scandals* featured abbreviated skirts that finally drove critic Percy Hammond to complain, "The knee is a joint, not an entertainment."

Audiences disagreed and made the producer a millionaire. Unlike *Ziegfeld's Follies*, White's *Scandals* gained special luster not from the chorus lines but from the melodic ones. George and Ira Gershwin wrote the *Scandals*' music, and their songs included "I'll Build a Stairway to Paradise" and "Somebody Loves Me." The songwriting trio of De Silva, Brown, and Henderson offered hits like "Life Is Just a Bowl of Cherries." Earl Carroll, a former songwriter, produced a series of *Vanities*, outdoing White by starring chorus girls in their underwear—and sometimes less.

To compensate for an exuberant lack of taste, Carroll presented first-rate comedians like Fields and Benny. Both men were fearless practitioners of their art—except when it came to one act. The two hated to appear with the Marx Brothers. In his memoirs, Fields commented, "They sang, danced, played the harp, and kidded in zany style, were vaudeville entertainers. Never saw so much nepotism or such hilarious laughter in my life. The only act I could never follow." Benny echoed: "My God, they did 35 minutes of their own stuff, and when my quiet act followed, it was disaster!" Nonetheless the Marxes did give him some benefits. "After a while I used to stand in the wings and laugh like hell; which meant I stopped worrying about my act."

Vaudeville remained big in the early twenties, but as the decade wound down, two inventions began to make fatal inroads: radio and films. By then Keith had died, and Albee had wrested control of the Palace from Martin Beck. Marcus Loew, onetime furrier and currently owner of a group of nickelodeons, had come on the scene, combining live acts and two-reelers at his New York showcase, Loew's State. The theater had well over three thousand seats, charged less than the Palace, and grossed more.

Unsettled, Albee ordered one of his ushers to buy a ticket at Loew's State as soon as the box office opened—and another just as it closed. Since the tickets had consecutive numbers, Albee could figure out exactly how many people had paid to get in. After a few weeks, someone figured out what the usher was doing and told Loew. He picked up his phone and twisted the knife: "Ed, you don't have to go to all that trouble. You can call up my house manager, and he will give you the box-office figures each day."

As late as 1927, the year of the first big sound film, *The Jazz Singer*, Marcus Loew still sounded eupeptic about vaudeville's fortunes. Invited to a Harvard seminar on movies, he spoke about the way he combined cinema and live performances at the State. Afterward he took questions:

> Q: Does a strong vaudeville act tend to bolster up a weak picture?

A: A great name will help bolster up what is lacking in a picture.
Q: Does broadcasting hurt your business any?
A: Not at all. The only time radio hurts is when there is a big fight on or some other occasion that makes everybody stay home and listen in. That particular night we are hurt.
Q: Is the Vitaphone going to cut into the vaudeville business in the near future?
A: That is hard to say. I put that on a par with anything else that is new. Personally, I do not think that it is.

If the emergence of the "talkies" reduced the opportunities for vaudevillians, the Great Depression shrank them even more. Edward Albee, the tight-fisted Mr. Vaudeville for so many years, himself fell victim to a hostile takeover by the Kennedy founding father, Joseph P. Kennedy. Expert at outmaneuvering businessmen, Kennedy sold off the Keith circuit and used the income to create the RKO movie studio. Albee, with a big office and nothing to do, kept burdening his new boss with suggestions, until Kennedy finally snapped: "Ed, don't you know you're all through?" The deflated executive retired to Florida and died in 1930.

Two years later vaudeville made its own way to the cemetery, when the Palace Theater relinquished its identity. Novelist and vaudeville aficionado Sarah Addison was there: "On a certain evening in May a few hundred New Yorkers attended a wake. The rites were held at the Palace Theater; the corpse was Vaudeville, being shown for the last time in the last two-a-day, reserved-seat, non-film vaudeville house in America. The authorities are pretty well convinced that the corpse is permanently dead.

"The house was embarrassingly empty, the orchestra seats not half filled. There was no funeral oration and there were no tears.

The performers were jolly, and the audience, scant as it was, was amused. Only a few lonely souls sat back in their seats mourning. Vaudeville, old-time, big-time vaudeville, had outlived its usefulness—the empty house certified to that—and its death carried no sting. The date was, incidentally, Friday the thirteenth."

Sophie Tucker agreed: "The movies have a death grip on vaudeville." And June Havoc, whose sister Gypsy Rose Lee became a headline stripper in burlesque, spoke for many colleagues: "Show business as I knew it had simply dwindled and vanished before my eyes. The happy island of vaudeville which had been my kindergarten, elementary and junior high school had sunk into the sea and left me treading water. . . . I was a displaced person."

Yet vaudeville has a lively ghost. From the late 1940s, when hardly anyone watched it, until the late 1960s, when almost everyone did, *The Ed Sullivan Show* carried on the vaudeville format on television, loading Sunday nights with pop singers and opera divas (the rarely seen Maria Callas performed an aria from *Tosca*) and a splendiferous variety of comedians, hoofers, singers, and performing seals. Like Flo Ziegfeld, who could neither sing, dance, nor play an instrument and yet produced the most enticing shows of his time, "Ed does nothing," Alan King quipped, "but he does it better than anyone else."

The public appetite for variety hasn't diminished. Stephen Sondheim once described his newly revived collage of vignettes, *Pacific Overtures*, as "documentary vaudeville." Jay Leno, David Letterman, and Conan O'Brien, taking cues from predecessors Jack Paar and Johnny Carson, have welcomed many a comic, singer, dancer, and juggler, Palace-style, though we call these programs "talk shows." You could even argue that the most obvious manifestation of the ghost is not the stage musical or such retro films as *Chicago* but the battery-powered remote. It allows potatoes to choose from a cascade of entertainment without leaving their couches, just as yesteryear's audiences did by sitting back and placing themselves in the hands of Albee, Keith, and Ziegfeld. "If vaudeville is dead," observes writer Larry Gelbart (*M**A*S**H**), "television is the box they put it in." Requiescat in video.

(CURTAIN)

The Americanization of Irving Berlin

It is supremely fitting that "God Bless America"—that stirring hymn to patriotism—has become our unofficial anthem in the aftermath of September 11, since the life of the legendary New York songsmith who penned it, Irving Berlin, born one Israel Baline in 1888 in distant Siberia, epitomizes everything about America's indomitable civilization that our terrorist enemies despise: its openness to striving and talent, its freedom, its inexhaustible optimism and creativity.

Baline's amazing American success story began when he stepped onto Ellis Island in 1893, on his way to Gotham's teeming Lower East Side, "the eyesore of New York and perhaps the filthiest place on the continent," according to the *New York Times* of the era. However dirty and poor, this Jewish ghetto was incubating an American renaissance that would produce legislators, merchants, professionals of all stripes—and Irving Berlin. Berlin's family was too poor to provide piano lessons, let alone a piano; Berlin would remain musically illiterate. His father, Moses, a cantor, gave him a love of melody and a quick wit, but that was about all he could afford. To supplement the family's meager income, Israel, more fluent in English than his parents and five older siblings, haggled with a nearby junk shop. "I used to go there selling bits and pieces of an old samovar that my mother had brought from Russia and kept under the bed," he once recalled. "I'd get five and ten cents for the pieces and kept selling them until the entire samovar disappeared."

Berlin understood the value of hard-earned money from early on. Hawking papers on a downtown pier in 1901, a thirteen-year-old Israel had just sold his fifth copy of the *New York Evening Journal* when a loading crane swung into his path, knocking him into the East River. Fished out just in time, he was given artificial respiration and packed off to Gouverneur Hospital for further ministrations. An hour later, as the young newsie slept, a nurse pried open his clenched hand. In it: five copper coins. He remained tightfisted for the rest of his 101 years.

Shortly after Israel was bar mitzvahed, Moses died, and the following year young Izzy left home and school to try his luck at street singing. Sans education, but brimming with aspiration and besotted with the street sounds and street language of the town he would never leave for long, the teenage Berlin plied his trade along the Bowery and the Lower East Side. He soon got a regular gig at the roughhouse Pelham Café, doing ribald parodies of popular hits. The salary was meager, but the café provided a piano and a place to hang out. He taught himself to play a bit by ear, amused the rowdy crowds, and picked up small change. A colleague, Jubal Sweet, remembered the young Berlin "moving around easy, singing all the time, every time a nickel would drop, he'd put his toe on it and kick it or nurse it to a certain spot. When he was done, he'd have all the jack in a pile, see?"

As the pile grew, Izzy kept his eye open for the main chance. It came in 1907 when a song in an Italian dialect, "My Mariucci Take a Steam Boat," swept through the saloons. Collaborating with a melodist, Izzy wrote the lyrics for "Marie from Sunny Italy," to be performed with the same Neapolitan intonation:

Please come out tonight my queen
Can't you hear my mandolin?

The riffraff made "Marie" a hit. Spurred by its success, Izzy Baline changed his name to Irving Berlin and began to write more songs—lots more. After all, if one ditty could earn a few coins, perhaps a hundred would make him rich. Berlin set to work, eighteen hours a day, seven days a week.

Right from the start, he shattered conventions. By contrast with the popular songs of his time, which used stilted language and wooden, overly refined images, Berlin resolved instead to use the rude wit and terse phrases of everyday speech. "Three-fourths of the quality which brings success to popular songs is phrasing," he later noted. "I make a study of it—ease, naturalness, every-day-ness—and it's my first consideration when I start on lyrics."

One early effort perfectly encapsulates Berlin's marvelously creative economy with words. Berlin took off from an actor's offhand remark that he was free for the evening because "my wife's in the country." "Now, the usual and unsuccessful way of handling a line like that," Berlin said, "is to dash off a jumble of verses about the henpecked husband, all leading up to a chorus running, we'll say, something like this:

My wife's gone to the country,
She went away last night.
Oh, I'm so glad! I'm so glad!
I'm crazy with delight!

Needlessly wordy and flat, thought Berlin. "All night I sweated to find what I knew was there, and I finally speared the lone word, just a single word, that made the song—and a fortune. Listen:

My wife's gone to the country!
Hooray!

"*Hooray*! That word gave the whole idea of the song in one quick wallop," enthused Berlin. "It gave the singer a chance to hoot with sheer joy. It invited the roomful to join in the hilarious shout." He concludes: "And I wasn't content until I had used my good thing to the limit. 'She took the children with her—Hooray! *Hooray*!'"

Berlin's early lyrics—now increasingly wrapped in melodies of his own invention—depicted the world of immigrant New York that he knew well, especially that of the avidly assimilating Jews. "Sadie Salome" concerns a young lady who takes to the stage, much to the consternation of her sweetheart, Moses:

Don't do that dance, I tell you, Sadie,
That's not a business for a lady!
Most ev'rybody knows
That I'm your loving Mose
Oy, oy, oy, oy
Where is your clothes?

"Business Is Business" explored the humorous crossroads where avarice and amour meet:

Business is business, Miss Rosie Cohen,
I've got to pay for everything I own
Seven suits of clothes your father took from my store,
All he says is "Charge it to my future son-in-law."
Tell your expensive father C.O.D.

Don't mean "Come On Down" to my store, for
Ev'ry little dollar carries int'rest of its own,
Bus'ness is business, Rosie Cohen!

Years later Berlin's contemporary, Groucho Marx, would sing these ethnic Jewish songs at parties, to the songwriter's excruciating embarrassment. "Every time I see him," Berlin grumbled, "I stick my hand in my pocket and ask him, 'How much if you don't sing it?'" It wasn't just his co-religionists whom Berlin sent up, however. The Bard of the Bowery was an equal-opportunity gadfly. For his Teutonic neighbors he wrote "Oh, How That German Could Love." For the Irish there was "Molly-O!" For blacks "Colored Romeo."

Not content with ethnic humor, Berlin began writing about sexual shenanigans too. Amused by the bawdy tales that young showgirls told their friends, he made this bold inquiry:

How do you do it, Mabel
On twenty dollars a week?
Tell us how you are able,
On twenty dollars a week,
A fancy flat and a diamond bar,
Twenty hats and a motorcar;
Go right to it,
But how do you do it,
On twenty dollars a week?

Had Berlin just stuck with ethnic jokes and ribaldry, he undoubtedly would have won big profits and a bright, if short-lived, reputation, like so many Tin Pan Alley writers of the time. But there was always something more ambitious about him. Where other songsmiths were personally flamboyant, he was fastidious, carefully barbered, turned out in the best suits he could afford. Where the others chased secretaries around desks, he dated women with politesse. Where the others were content with hack-work that the public gobbled up like peanuts, he wanted to serve up more substantial fare.

Berlin's higher aspirations made him alert to changes in the cultural atmosphere—like jazz. His composition "Alexander's Ragtime Band" wasn't really a rag, rather a song *about* rag, but that was good enough for sheet-music buyers, who in 1911 made it their Number One choice in the United States and abroad. To his astonishment, Irving Berlin became a brand name on both sides of the Atlantic. The song has remained popular until today, with a time out during the Vietnam War. For sixties protesters, one couplet crystallized all that was wrong with Amerika:

They can play a bugle call like you never heard before
So natural that you want to go to war. . . .

In 1912, fresh from his "Alexander" success, Berlin experienced both great happiness and profound loss. He married Dorothy Goetz, sister of a fellow songwriter. After a traditional Jewish wedding, the couple sailed off to honeymoon in the Caribbean. Typhoid had hit the region; Dorothy contracted it. Five months later she was dead. The Berlin song factory shut down.

It wasn't until the following year that Berlin mastered his grief; unsurprisingly, he came to terms with it in a song dedicated to his bride's memory:

I lost the sunshine and roses
I lost the heavens of blue . . .
I lost the angel who gave me
Summer the whole winter through
I lost the gladness

That turned into sadness,
When I lost you.

He never wrote so autobiographically again; his life remained creatively off-limits.

From then on until late in the century, the song factory ran at full capacity. Some songs took the writer weeks of concentrated effort; others he scribbled in taxis or composed tossing restlessly in bed. Past triumphs evaporated as soon as he started to work; each song, he later admitted, came to life "under a nervous strain, and more often than otherwise I feel as if my life depends on my accomplishing a song." Note: not writing or composing, *accomplishing*. Because of the effort required, Berlin never slept much; barbiturates were one of his basic food groups.

It was after Dorothy's death that another theme began to emerge in Berlin's life and writing: a deep love of the country that had allowed such success. "Patriotism," notes biographer Laurence Bergreen, "was Irving Berlin's true religion. It evoked the same emotional response in him that conventional religion summoned in others; it was his rock."

In 1915, shortly after becoming an American citizen, Berlin offered an early expression of his patriotism, "The International Rag," a song that derided those Europeans who lamented the influence of U.S. dress, idioms, and music. Contemporary European America-bashers could still learn from it:

What did you do, America?
They're after you, America.
You got excited and started something,
Nations jumping all around;
You've got a lot to answer for,
They lay the blame right at your door. . . .

Looking around his beloved adopted nation, Berlin saw that one benefit of its burgeoning prosperity was progress in educating ever-greater numbers of people. He regretted his own lack of schooling and set out in what spare time he had "to at least get a bowing acquaintance with the world's best literature, and some knowledge of history, and all of the famous dead people." In addition to Shakespeare, whose expensively bound works he displayed in his home, Berlin loved American history and culture. He treasured his autographed first editions of American novels and a biography of Abraham Lincoln that came with some of the president's letters.

As Berlin's love for America deepened, so did his interest in politics. When World War I first engulfed the Old World, Berlin took a pacifist stance, but in 1917 he sharply reversed course:

Lincoln, Grant and Washington,
They were peaceful men, each one;
Still they took the sword and gun
When real trouble came,
And I feel somehow
They are wond'ring now
If we'll do the same.

The following year found Private Irving Berlin drafted. His musical plaint still rings out at military bases around the world:

Someday I'm going to murder the bugler;
Someday they're going to find him dead—
I'll amputate his reveille,
And step upon it heavily. . . .

Other composers would've stopped there. Not Berlin. He was forever in search of the "kicker"—the final line that summed up a song and made the audience smile. In the last chorus, he fingered the true culprit:

And then I'll get that other pup,
The one who wakes the bugler up,
And spend the rest of my life in bed.

For an army show at Camp Yaphank, Berlin wrote another song, then put it back in his trunk: "God Bless America" wouldn't see daylight for twenty years, but it perfectly expressed Berlin's patriotic feelings at the time and later.

Given Berlin's pro-democracy, pro–United States worldview, it's no surprise that he was one of the first popular artists to skewer the new Soviet Socialist Republic. He used his kicker to warn Americans, "Look Out for the Bolsheviki Man":

To the speeches that he makes
Tie a little can;
He hasn't got a single sou,
And he wants to share it all with you. . . .

In case anyone missed the point, Berlin followed with "The Revolutionary Rag":

'Twas made across the sea
By a tricky, slicky, Bolsheviki.
Run with your little moneybag
Or else they'll steal it all away, wheel it all away,
As they go raving, madly waving
That Revolutionary Rag.
It's not a melody.
It's a crimson flag. . . .

Berlin didn't just defend American democracy from its enemies; he also cast a perceptive eye on changes in social mores on the home front. Splitsville, an area rarely visited in the prewar period, became a favorite subject. "A Fair Exchange Scene" caricatures wife- and husband-swapping in the Jazz Age:

JUDGE: *What do you want?*
COUPLE: *A divorce.*
JUDGE: *Do you really want it?*
COUPLE: *Of course!*
JUDGE: *Are you tired of him? And you of her?*
COUPLE: *We'd rather not discuss it, sir!*
JUDGE: *But you must have a very good reason—And you cannot keep it mum.*
COUPLE: *We have two very good reasons—And here they come!*
(Enter the SECOND COUPLE*)*

Hollywood bluenoses, prohibition, the loose morals of Greenwich Village, religion—hardly any American phenomenon was outside his ambit.

The year 1925 marked a watershed in Berlin's life: he met the young—sixteen years his junior—socialite Ellin Mackay, a Catholic. The two fell instantly in love, infuriating her father, who was president of Western Union. He forbade the courtship and even sent Ellin on a European trip so that she'd forget about her show-business upstart. This, of course, was the stuff of tabloids, and the *New York Mirror* ran a slew of stories (some actually true) about the couple. "The day you marry my daughter," Clarence Mackay allegedly told Berlin, "I'll disinherit her." Berlin supposedly retorted, "The day I marry your daughter, I'll settle $2 million on her." Another reported clash had Mackay boasting of his ancestry, and Berlin countering, "I can trace mine back to Exodus." Said Mackay: "Is that so? Here's another Exodus for you. Get out."

The composer gave his wife a unique present upon their marriage at City Hall in 1926: the song "Always." In later years George S. Kaufman, director of the Marx Brothers' first show, *The Cocoanuts*, claimed that Berlin wanted to shoehorn the number into it. Kaufman, perhaps recalling his own peccadilloes, grumbled that the verse was unrealistic. "Instead of 'I'll be loving you, Always,'" he said, "it should be 'I'll be loving you, Thursday.'"

When the depression came the Berlins stayed in the headlines and out of the breadlines. Hit followed hit in the early 1930s; royalty checks flooded in. In 1933, writer and director Moss Hart seized on Berlin's ability to turn current events into profitable songs. The collaboration resulted in *As Thousands Cheer*, a Broadway revue built around newspaper headlines. Herbert Hoover, leaving the White House to a Bronx cheer, Mahatma Gandhi sitting cross-legged on a mat, Josephine Baker caterwauling, Walter Winchell retailing gossip—Berlin's songs poked fun at them all.

Not everything in the revue was satirical, however. Those who had dismissed Berlin as a lightweight changed their tune when Ethel Waters appeared in a powerful scene with the headline UNKNOWN NEGRO LYNCHED BY FRENZIED MOB. The writer had produced more than his share of "coon songs"—comic numbers in black dialect—and most people assumed he would carry on in that style. Instead he underwent a change of attitude twenty years before his country did, and gave Waters "Supper Time." The piece brought down the house every night:

Kids will soon be yellin'
For their supper time;
How'll I keep from tellin' that
That man o' mine
Ain't comin' home no more?

How'll I keep explainin'
When they ask me where he's gone?
How'll I keep from cryin'
When I bring their supper on?

Berlin wasn't content to editorialize in song: his deeds backed up his belief in racial equality. During the rehearsals, actors Clifton Webb and Helen Broderick refused to take curtain calls alongside a Negro. Very well, responded Berlin, no one would bow for any number. The mutiny promptly ended; thereafter all three performers acknowledged the applause together.

Had the composer retired in the early 1930s, he'd be remembered as two Irving Berlins—the writer of "singles," songs that went out and succeeded on their own; and the creator of words and music for Broadway revues. But there were more Berlins to come. A third sojourned in Hollywood, a place that he found three thousand miles too far from Manhattan. It did have one incomparable asset, however: Fred Astaire.

When Jerome Kern said, "Astaire *can't* do anything bad," Berlin concurred. "You give Fred Astaire a song," he observed, "and you could forget about it. If he did change anything, he made it better." No wonder almost all the great New York songwriters of the period trekked out West to work with the dancer, among them Kern, Johnny Mercer, and Cole Porter. It was an extraordinary confluence of craftsmen and artists. Unlike the others, Berlin had no formal musical training or schooling, yet the autodidact more than held his own. By every critical measure, *Top Hat* is the greatest of the Fred Astaire–Ginger Rogers collaborations, boasting such Berlin classics as "Isn't This a Lovely Day to Be Caught in the Rain?" "Cheek to Cheek," and the title tune, which established Astaire's jaunty protagonist in a series of cascading rhymes:

I'm
Dudin' up my shirt front,
Puttin' in the shirt studs,
Polishin' my nails.
I'm steppin' out, my dear,
To breathe an atmosphere
That simply reeks with class;
And I trust
That you'll excuse my dust
When I step on the gas
For I'll be there
Puttin' down my top hat,
Messin' up my white tie,
Dancin' in my tails.

Now that Berlin moved in fast company—in every sense—he quickened the tempo of many numbers and raised his craft to a higher level, ready to match wits with the great Cole Porter himself. Indeed, he wrote a private salute to his fellow Astaire fan, kidding "You're the Top":

You're the top!
You're Miss Pinkham's tonic
You're the top!
You're a high colonic;
You're the burning heat of a bridal suite in use,
You're the breasts of Venus,
You're King Kong's penis,
You're self-abuse.

The proof was there for anyone to see and hear: Berlin's verbal agility could match even that of Yale grad and musical scholar Porter.

Berlin never minded reaching into his trunk and taking out an old number when the time was ripe. And the epoch of the Munich Conference was *over*ripe. Shortly after Neville Chamberlain & Co. acceded to Hitler's demand for the Sudetenland, Berlin added a few touches to "God Bless America" and published it to national acclaim.

Republicans asked to use the song at their 1940 convention; so did the Democrats. Although for years, Berlin—concerned by high taxes and swelling government—had been moving inexorably from left to right (he rooted for Wendell Willkie to unseat President Roosevelt), he chose to sidestep controversy and let both parties use the song. Within months, "God Bless America" became so popular that the composer felt uncomfortable when the enormous royalties rolled in: this was, after all, a piece extolling patriotism, not a Broadway production designed for gain. In a bold philanthropic gesture—though he hated squandering money, he was generous if the cause was right—he ceded the profits in perpetuity to the Boy Scouts and Girl Scouts.

Enthusiasts lobbied to replace the difficult "Star Spangled Banner" with words a child could recall and a tune the tone-deaf could carry. Flattered but abashed, the writer answered, "We've got a good national anthem. You can't have two." True enough; but there was no law about having an *unofficial* national anthem, and "God Bless America" became the people's choice—as it has become again post–September 11.

Berlin wrote other anthems that made it into the national bloodstream, as Philip Roth noted with typical salinity. In *Operation Shylock*, the narrator observes, "God gave Moses the 10 Commandments, and He gave to Irving Berlin 'Easter Parade' and 'White Christmas.' The two holidays that celebrate the divinity of Christ—the divinity that's the very heart of the Jewish rejection of

Christianity—and what does Irving Berlin do? Easter he turns into a fashion show and Christmas into a holiday about snow."

In fact, Irving and Ellin raised all three of their daughters as Protestants. They sent them to tony private schools as well, and Ellin saw to it that they observed the amenities. She also made sure the trio recognized who had given them their penthouse on East End Avenue. When Linda was very young, she remembered, Mama instructed her to get her elbows off the dinner table. "But Daddy has *his* elbows on the table," the child complained. "That's different," instructed Ellin. "Your father is a genius."

Few would have disputed her—certainly no one in uniform during World War II. When the hostilities began, Berlin turned his attention to the armed services. He recruited talent from the ranks for a touring show, *This Is the Army*, and donated profits from the musical to the Army Emergency Relief Fund. The production offered more than twenty new Berlin songs, including one for black troops—thus creating, willy-nilly, the army's first integrated unit.

The show toured Great Britain just as Prime Minister Winston Churchill was reading war dispatches by the brilliant Oxford don Isaiah Berlin, at the time head of the Special Survey Section of the British Embassy in Washington. Churchill asked for a meeting. A communications snafu sent the luncheon invitation to the wrong I. Berlin, and Irving showed up at Number 10. The PM addressed him as Professor and grilled him about the progress of the war. Bewildered, the composer answered in monosyllables until a frustrated Churchill gave up and turned to the guest on his left. Later he commented: "Berlin's like most bureaucrats. Wonderful on paper, but disappointing when you meet them face to face."

Composer Jerome Kern, who knew the difference between Berlins, was wiser. Asked about Irving's place in American music at this time, he answered: "To my mind, there are phrases in Berlin's music as noble and mighty as any clause in the works of the Masters, from Beethoven and Wagner on down." In short, "Irving Berlin has no place in American music. He is American music."

Irving had proved that movie musicals presented no obstacle, but Broadway was different. Although Berlin had been a star composer in the days of the Follies, the theater had undergone vast alterations since then. Replacing the old revues and girlie extravaganzas, "book shows" now used songs to define character and propel plot. Gotham's Great White Way was home to such colossi as Leonard Bernstein, George and Ira Gershwin, Rodgers and Hammerstein, Kurt Weill, and two gentlemen who, like Berlin, dared to write their own words *and* music, Harold Rome and the British visitor Noel Coward. Could Irving Berlin compete?

He'd give it his best shot in 1945. Replacing Kern, who had died while *Annie Get Your Gun* was in preparation, Berlin turned the romance of Annie Oakley and Buffalo Bill into a credible backstage story. En route, he showed that at age fifty-seven he hadn't lost the ability to tell a joke in verse. Some of the biggest laughs came from a chorus of one- and two-syllable words, adhering to Berlin's ideal of economy of expression:

My uncle out in Texas
Can't even write his name;
He signs his check with X's,
But they cash them all the same.

Nor had he lost his gift for anthems—this one dedicated to show business:

There's no people like show people;
They smile when they are low.
Yesterday they told you you would not go far,

That night you open and there you are,
Next day on your dressing room they've hung a star—
Let's go on with the show.

Total: forty-five words—forty-one of one syllable, three of two syllables, one of three syllables.

The Master stumbled, though, with *Miss Liberty*, a musical about the statue of the same name. Then, just when the critics were set to treat him as a relic, he returned with *Call Me Madam* in 1950. This SRO smash was based loosely on the life and times of Perle Mesta, Washington's then "Hostess with the Mostest." Berlin came up with a series of sparklers, including "Marrying for Love."

One new song, however, sparked more enthusiasm than the others. "They Like Ike" (converted to "I Like Ike" for the presidential campaign of 1952) was Irving's hymn to a fellow conservative. Once again, Berlin used simplicity, coupled with an unpredictable kicker, to make his point:

A leader we can call
Without political noise,
He can lead us all
As he led the boys.
Let's take Ike,
A man we all of us like,
Tried and true,
Courageous, strong and human—
Why, even Harry Truman
Says "I Like Ike."

Thousands of undecided voters may have found themselves persuaded when they heard the song ring out during the televised GOP convention of 1952. The convert who meant the most to

Berlin, though, was his wife: a lifelong Democrat, Ellin signed a newspaper ad testifying that she too liked Ike.

After the 1952 campaign, Berlin mostly kept his politics offstage. Still, when the spirit moved him, he'd rebuke those who needed a lesson in Americanism. Lyricist E. Y. "Yip" Harburg, a splenetic member of the Old Left, got under Berlin's thin skin during the Vietnam War by sarcastically recommending that "God Bless America" be retitled "God Help America." Berlin proposed new verses for the song:

God bless America,
Land I enjoy,
No discussions with Russians
Till they stop sending arms to Hanoi. . . .
God bless America
When skies are dark,
God bless America,
My Noah's ark.

Irving Berlin sailed in his beloved ark to the age of 101. Before his death in 1989 there were multitudinous awards, ranging from presidential citations to a Carnegie Hall recital celebrating his life's work. And there was, of course, the limitless ocean of royalties. But there were also many sorrows before the final curtain descended.

Irving's last Broadway show, *Mr. President*, bombed. Ellin died in 1988, in the sixty-second year of their marriage, after which Berlin rarely ventured out of his East Side digs. He lived to see his oeuvre drowned out by the din of rock 'n' roll, with its celebration of the singer, not the song. And he watched as love for one's country became cringe-making within the academy, the High Journalism, and the Beltway.

Yet honest craft and valid emotion have a way of outlasting fashion. In the last several years, cabaret singers have revived the Berlin masterworks; there are now more than thirty CDs celebrating his work, ranging from Ella Fitzgerald's classic renditions to Michael Feinstein's friskier tributes. A beautiful book, *The Collected Lyrics of Irving Berlin*, is edited with impeccable scholarship by Robert Kimball. And of course, there's been "God Bless America." Irving Berlin's sentiments have proven their lasting worth. As he observed,

A fiddler can speak with his fiddle.
A singer can speak with his voice,
An actor can speak
With his tongue in his cheek,
But a songwriter has no choice.
Whatever his rights or his wrongs,
He can only speak with his songs.

There are almost a thousand of those speeches in the *Collected Lyrics*, each a time capsule of our manners and mores, our shifting identities and permanent values. No one has ever been so concise, or so consistent, about why America remains our home sweet home.

The Yiddish Theater's Triumph

On a pleasant June evening in 1906, Manhattan's original odd couple strolled down Second Avenue. The tall man with black beard and dark, deep-set eyes was playwright Jacob Gordin, the Yiddish theater's first great realist and a dominant presence on the Lower East Side. Speaking with big gestures, the Russian immigrant went on about socialism, his eight children, his adaptations of Shakespeare, his interpretations of Tolstoy's thought.

Gordin's older companion, returned to his native America after a twenty-year absence, was a dedicated novelist, master of nuance, lifelong bachelor, apolitical, bald, clean-shaven of late, tentative in style and speech, as Gentile in his way as the other was Jewish. The playwright led the way and chattered on; Henry James did the sightseeing.

What he apprehended did not seem encouraging. All around him was the pulse of cultural life, the voracious appetite for technical knowledge and dramatic art—the very art at which James had failed so publicly in London. But the great observer, his aural and olfactory senses besieged and affronted, couldn't see what spread out before him. The cafés, filled with folk speaking in accented, ungrammatical English, were "torture-rooms of the living idiom." This "Hebrew conquest of New York," James felt certain, would permanently maim the language. In the future, "whatever we shall know it for, certainly we shall not know it for English." The Yiddish theater, to which his companion had politely escorted him, was equally cringe-making. James fled after the first act of an operetta, not because it was incomprehensible—Gordin explained the plotline as it went along—but because its audience offended. Those ticket buyers emanated "a scent, literally, not further to be followed."

Other WASP tourists were not so fastidious. Praising Jewish immigration as the great hope of New York, Lincoln Steffens, editor of the muckraking *Commercial Advertiser*, told his readers that he considered himself "almost a Jew." He felt as infatuated with the Lower East Side as adolescents were with the Wild West, nailed a mezuzah on his office door, and every year on Yom Kippur spent the whole twenty-four hours fasting and visiting synagogues around the city.

Hutchins Hapgood, the paper's star reporter, did his boss one better. The thirty-something Harvard blueblood, whose family had settled in Massachusetts in 1656, celebrated downtown Jewry in a clothbound best-seller. *The Spirit of the Ghetto* compared the Lower East Side with quattrocento Florence: "Altogether there is an excitement in ideas and an enthusiastic energy for acquiring knowledge which has an interesting analogy to the hopefulness and acquisitive desire of the early Renaissance." It was, Hapgood believed, "a mistake to think that the young Hebrew turns naturally to trade. He turns his energy to whatever offers the best opportunity for broader life and success. Other things besides business are open to him in this country."

The most significant of those things, in Hapgood's view, was the Yiddish theater. The journalist did not exit from productions at intermission but stayed to observe a rapt audience, most of whom had never before seen a drama or comedy of any kind. (The nearest many had come to a theatrical experience was the *Purimspiel*, a yearly masque at temples, celebrating the biblical account of Queen Esther's triumph over the wicked anti-Semite Haman.)

The theaters themselves, on or close to Second Avenue, the aorta of the ghetto, were smaller versions of those uptown, the visitor noted, with chandeliers and balconies and flies for the scenery. The seat holders could be as boisterous as a crowd at the Elizabethan Globe or as hypnotized as children at a pantomime. The fare comprised serious works as well as *shund*—the Yiddish term for blatantly commercial melodrama: stories of wayward wives, drunken husbands, cruel landlords, children who married "no-goods," and so on. Hapgood attended them all, keeping a close eye on the actors and a closer one on the onlookers, observing "the sweat-shop woman with her baby, the day laborer, the Russian-Jewish anarchist and socialist, the Ghetto rabbi and scholar, the poet, the journalist." To him, as to so many of the fugitives from Eastern European pogroms, the Yiddish theater seemed to have a past as deep as Jewish history. In fact, it was younger than Hapgood himself.

The historical language of the Jews was, of course, Hebrew, the sanctified tongue of the Bible and prayer. Yiddish was the common speech of an ever-mobile people. It took form in the tenth century as a fusion of the Jewish-French dialect Laaz with Middle High German, mixing in new phrases from the various "Jew Streets" of major Western European cities. As the Jews drifted north and east to Poland and the Ukraine, where the tsars suffered them to live, they picked up more expressions from the Slavic tongues. Written in Hebrew script, Yiddish was a living language, pronounced with great expression and musical cadence.

Anecdotes sprang up, stories that found a home in the wry attitude and rapid pulse of Yiddish: Two Jews decide to assassinate the tsar. They bring sharp knives and conceal themselves behind trees in a park where the Russian leader takes his daily stroll. Hours pass, and the tsar fails to appear. At sundown one of them worries: "I hope nothing happened to him."

One Jew sighs to another, "It would be best never to have been born." His friend agrees: "True, but how many are that lucky? Maybe one in a hundred thousand."

Two Jews face execution by a firing squad. The captain offers Sol and Mendel blindfolds. Sol accepts. Mendel spits in the officer's face: "Keep your lousy blindfold!" Sol demurs: "Mendel, don't make trouble!"

As a magnificent funeral procession passes by the shtetl gates an old man weeps. "You're a relative?" asks an astonished friend. "No." "Then how come you're crying?" "That's why."

With all its richness of attitude and lore, the language did not please everyone who spoke it. In *The Joys of Yiddish*, Leo Rosten notes that purists derided Yiddish for its "bastard" origins, its "vulgar" idioms, its "hybrid" vocabulary. Russians called it "*zhargon*"; Germans condemned it as a "barbarous argot." Worse still, Hebraicists thought it "uncivilized cant." The greatest of them, the eighteenth-century scholar Moses Mendelssohn, wrote in German, stressed secular knowledge and social assimilation, and encouraged his co-religionists to speak in the tongues of their host countries. Yiddish, he declared, was "ridiculous, ungrammatical and a cause of moral corruption."

On his counsel, many Jews did learn the tongues of other nations. Yet they stubbornly clung to Yiddish as the *mamaloshen*—the mother tongue. In a cascade of irony, Mendelssohn became revered as a scholar and philosopher but lost his place as a guardian of the Jewish spirit. His grandson, the composer Felix Mendelssohn-Bartholdy, was raised a Christian and had no memory of synagogue attendance, nor had most of Felix's cousins. Meantime the children of the mother tongue kept their traditions and retained their religion.

By the nineteenth century, Eastern European Jews had been speaking Yiddish for many centuries and knew it as well as they knew any other language. The Goldfaden family of Odessa was typical. Transformed by the Enlightenment (*Haskalah* in Hebrew), they spoke fluent Russian, French, and German—yet the *mamaloshen* was the language they spoke at home. They sent their brightest child, Abraham, to a progressive Jewish academy, where his teachers encouraged him to read Western literature and to study the Talmud and the Torah. But he too felt most comfortable speaking and writing Yiddish.

After graduation the well-educated but unfocused youth set out to find his destiny in Russia. Although musically illiterate, Goldfaden had a great ear; the tunes he banged out on the piano with two fingers caught the attention of local publishers and became hugely popular in Eastern European ghettos. With few copyright laws in effect, though, the royalties amounted to pennies. He became a teacher. When that career failed to satisfy, he tried retailing. Too few ladies came to his hat shop, however, and he pushed on to medical school in Vienna. But his mind wandered. Journalism suddenly exerted an appeal; this, he decided, was the proper occupation for the Coming Man.

Back in Russia, Goldfaden founded several Yiddish periodicals. One by one they went under. He headed for the boomtown of Jassy, Romania. Perhaps there, in a town full of progressive Jews, he could start a new paper. Upon arrival, Goldfaden dropped into a wine cellar called the Green Tree, where, astonished, he heard one of his own numbers performed by a popular singer. Afterward Goldfaden fantasized about something unheard of: a theater for Jews, just like those for Gentiles. "Out of this," his memoir states, "came a piece—a nonsense, a hodge-podge! I don't even recall the name of it!" Nevertheless, on October 5 and 9, 1876, at the Green Tree, Goldfaden's unremembered musical farce went on, performed by the professional singers he had hired, and applauded by a vociferous crowd.

Not a soul—including the father—knew that the Yiddish theater had just been born.

Moving from strength to strength, Goldfaden gathered a company of enthusiastic amateurs, wrote more plays and music, relocated to the Romanian capital, Bucharest, and toured the big cities and provinces of Eastern Europe. His success encouraged other Yiddish companies to spring up. Heading up one was Jacob Adler, a young businessman-turned-actor, who nourished his own dream of replacing *shund* with a higher, more artistic theater.

Tsar Alexander III—who blamed the 1881 assassination of his father, Alexander II, on laxity and liberalism—put a stop to all that. In the recent past the authorities had allowed religious Jews to grow more insular and had unwisely permitted their secular brothers to embrace socialism or Zionism. This would not do. A three-pronged solution to the "Jewish problem" went into effect: one-third conversion to Christianity, one-third emigration, and one-third starvation. Almost incidentally, on August 2, 1883, a decree went up in every town square in Russia: Yiddish theater henceforward would be illegal throughout the land.

Most of the impresarios and actors were unwilling to convert. None intended to stop eating. That left emigration. Goldfaden stayed behind, moving his company around in Eastern Europe, picking up small change in Romania and Poland. But the majority of Yiddish troupers bought steerage tickets to the Promised City: New York, New York, where they found thousands upon thousands of fellow refugees struggling for survival in a Lower East Side that soon grew more crowded than Calcutta's slums. Yet in spite (and because) of those conditions, the Jewish population thirsted for art and entertainment. The people of the Yiddish theater strove to give them both.

In the beginning came the actors, extravagant personalities who made their histrionic uptown equivalents—Edwin Booth, Eleanor Duse, the Barrymores—seem self-effacing. The first superstar started as a boy soprano. In the early 1880s, Boris Thomashefsky won a featured role in *Koldunya*, a Goldfaden operetta previously staged in Romania. When the diva failed to show on opening night, Boris crammed himself into her wig and dress and went onstage in the role. The Lower East Side crowd gave him a standing ovation. From that night on, Thomashefsky was a force to reckon with. By twenty-one, he was a married barnstormer, touring with his own company nine months of the year. Boris's father, Pincus, who had never written a word before, became the resident playwright. Once he had the plot, recalled Thomashefsky's wife, Bessie, "Boris and his father filled in the prose. Music they scratched together from other plays. Boris wrote one or two songs, and in three days' time, father and son were ready with a new 'masterpiece' for the Yiddish theater."

Too often those masterpieces lacked proper conclusions—Pincus liked to see his son improvise. "*Nu*," he would taunt. "You're supposed to be a star. Let's see how you'll end the play. I have to write everything out for you?" As a matter of fact, he didn't. Boris was a great ad-libber and a born crowd-pleaser. Inventing himself and his material as he went along, he became a celebrity in the Jewish areas of Baltimore, Philadelphia, and Detroit, and then moved back to the Lower East Side, billing himself "America's Darling."

A Yiddish poem dedicated to Boris (and reprinted in his theatrical programs) included the lines: "Thomashefsky! Artist great! No praise is good enough for you. You remain the king of the stage. Everything falls at your feet." Among the fallen objects was a throng of enraptured women, some of whom would faint when Boris made his bare-chested entrances in flesh-colored tights, barely acknowledging the audible swoons. When he played Solomon, the Second Avenue wags said that the only difference between the actor and the biblical king was that Solomon had to support his harem, whereas Boris's harem supported him.

The other items that fell at Thomashefsky's feet were coins—and he spent them all. In his self-celebrating but oddly revealing biography, *My Life Story*, written when he was reduced to singing for small change at a downtown nightclub, he remembers his competitors in the Yiddish theater. "If David Kessler wore a big hat with a long feather, Jacob Adler wore a bigger hat with three feathers and a gold scarf. I piled on colored stockings, coats, crowns, swords, shields, bracelets, earrings, turbans. Next to me, they looked like common soldiers. If they rode in on a real horse, I had a golden chariot drawn by two horses. If they killed an enemy, I killed an army."

Thomashefsky's greatest rival was a very different, and far more gifted, artist. In his own memoir, Jacob Adler admits, "I was weak as a singer. I had not a good voice nor, I confess it, a very good ear. But is this why I turned from the operetta to purely dramatic plays? I think not. From my earliest years I leaned toward those plays where the actor works not with jests and comic antics, but with the principles of art; not to amuse the public with tumbling, but to awaken in them and in himself the deepest and most powerful emotions."

In some ways Adler was astonishingly puritanical for his time. A fellow actor remarked in awe: "Jacob Adler never drank, never touched tobacco, never touched cards. Theater!" On the other hand, there were women, and with Jacob, that other hand was always straying. Two wives left their husbands for him, and he enjoyed innumerable liaisons. Assessing his personal relationships, Adler's own granddaughter wrote, "Truly, he was a cause of grief to every woman who loved him."

But he was also the lodestar of every production he ever graced, a performer of great acumen and charisma.

The third of the Yiddish theater's powerful triumvirate, David Kessler, was a bull of a man who could make ingenues and male actors burst into tears when he bawled them out for some trivial error. His idea of motivation was rage, followed by grudging admiration: "May he burn," he reportedly once said after putting a terrified performer through the wringer, "but the son of a bitch really played that scene." Assessed by Hapgood as "one of the best in dramatic roles, and one of the worst in musical ones," Kessler feared no one—except his wife, who kept women away from the stage door and, some said, made her husband do the household chores.

Although not a subtle actor, Kessler had the instincts of an artist and resented the lightweight, heavily costumed roles he had to play in order to maintain long lines at the box office. "All day long I am a human being," he complained. "I speak like a human being, act like a human being. At night I must dress myself up like a turkey, like an idiot! If I went out in the street like this people would throw stones at me for a lunatic. Here they shout bravo!"

Conflicts among these three were inevitable. For a brief period, Adler and Thomashefsky lived at 85 West Tenth Street—Jacob and his family on the first floor, Boris and his wife and children on the second. Adler's morning routine never varied. After ablutions he would stick his head in the dumbwaiter shaft and holler, "Thomashefsky, a black year on your head! Thomashefsky, the devil himself go into your bones!" Boris, amused at this routine, never responded. Let the downstairs neighbor go through his exercise; everyone knew who drew the bigger crowds, the larger salary.

Once, and once only, Adler, Kessler, and Thomashefsky appeared together in a performance. Kessler upstaged Thomashefsky late in the play, aping the younger man's broad gestures. Boris caught the stage business in the corner of his eye. The scene called for him to break a plate; furious, he smashed two. Staying within character, Kessler, who wasn't supposed to touch the plates, broke four. Partisans in the audience cheered on their favorites. Adler was playing a mild-mannered rabbi, but he had no intention of missing out on the excitement. He broke some plates himself. The others shattered more crockery. At the finale, shards of china covered the floor, and Adler, Kessler, and Thomashefsky were starting in on a table and chairs when the curtain came down.

The actors' competition had its echo in the Yiddish theater's writer wars. One of the most spectacular examples of *shund*—*Rashi, or the Persecution of the Jews in France*—was written by Moishe Isaac Halevy Hurwitz, an extraordinary hustler who could only have been produced overseas, and who could only have flourished in America.

Early on, the playwright learned of Abraham Goldfaden's efforts in Jassy. One afternoon a short, thickset visitor, bearded and dressed *à la mode*, presented himself backstage. He claimed to be the renowned Professor Hurwitz, specialist in world geography and playwriting. Something did not seem kosher, and Goldfaden asked a few questions around town. The "professor," it turned out, had once taught Hebrew school on the elementary level but soon got fired. He converted to Christianity and was currently a missionary in Bucharest. Confronted with the facts, Hurwitz acknowledged that he had indeed abandoned his old faith. "Hard times," he explained. "I didn't earn much with the old God. The new one brought me 90 francs a month." A man may do what he likes, Goldfaden told him, but there was no way a Jewish audience could accept the work of a Christian missionary.

Hurwitz thought this judgment arbitrary and biased, and stomped off. But the success of Goldfaden's troupe made him think twice about possibilities in the Yiddish theater. Over the next few weeks he gathered a minyan. Before these ten Jewish witnesses he pronounced himself a Hebrew once more, hired a bunch of amateur actors, and began to stage his own plays in the back room of a Romanian restaurant. Hurwitz turned up in London in the mid-1880s and made his way to the Lower East Side just in time for the birth of New York's Yiddish theater. There he ground out play after play, some plagiarized, some original, without breaking a sweat.

His main rival was the inspired hack Joseph Lateiner, a former prompter and translator in Goldfaden's troupe. It was Lateiner's custom, as one scholar put it, "to take a foreign play, squeeze every drop of juice out of it, change the Gentile names to Jewish ones, slap on manly beards and *peyes* [sidelocks] and let them parade across the stage as Jews."

But at least Lateiner tried to adhere to historical truth. Hurwitz had no standards at all; his strength was speed. The professor's "history plays" became notorious for mixing the events of two centuries, and he falsified events whenever it suited him. Once, in a self-created emergency, he cast himself as a sultan in an oriental drama. The purpose: to save the final act, incomplete on opening night. "Whatever I say, nod your head," he hissed to the company just before the curtain rose. Hurwitz came onstage and spouted high-sounding phrases for forty-five minutes. The others dutifully murmured assent, and as the curtain lowered the audience clapped and cheered as if it had all made sense.

Lateiner valiantly attempted to keep up. At first he wrote of the past, then thought to trump the competition with a story ripped from the headlines. His most earnest effort was *Tisla Eslar*, the true story of a rabbi recently accused of ritual murder in Hungary. The Lateiner play had just started its run when the rapid Hurwitz came up with *two* works on the same subject, *The Trial at Tisla Eslar* and *The Conspiracy at Tisla Eslar*. These would debut on successive nights, a first for the Yiddish theater.

Ironically, as theater historian Nahma Sandrow points out, the harder Lateiner and Hurwitz worked to accent their differences, the more the public linked them. Together they became "synonymous with vulgar dramatic baked goods of an uncertain freshness." Both "plunged into the bakery business, until the two were almost continually bent over their respective ovens like cartoon madmen, jerkily kneading and shoveling in play after play after play." Yet their works continued to draw audiences; no matter how bizarre the plots, how filled with sordid family squabbles, the ghetto dwellers regarded them as a form of documentary.

With good reason. For what the crowds saw onstage wasn't very different from what they witnessed in real life. Looking back, Boris Thomashefsky's son Teddy said that the world of the Yiddish theater "made the Left Bank of Paris look like a convent. There was every form of degeneration you can imagine: murder, suicide, drugs, sex deviations of all kinds. These were the emergent Jews, after living a Torah-cloistered existence, suddenly free—and drunk with it." Naturally, that degeneration made for the melodrama actors relished and audiences adored, laughing and weeping through what the theaters advertised as "two hours of solid entertainment."

Producers assumed that *shund* would always win out over serious drama. They referred to the public by the code name of "Moishe" (Moses), a caricature of the uncritical, easily amused ticket buyer who wanted everything to be histrionic and highly colored. Yet Moishe was not as simple as they thought. An inspired clown named Sigmund Mogulesco showed the Lower East Side that comedy could be subtle and informative; Hapgood called him "a natural genius of spontaneity." The actor never went for cheap laughs as the lesser comedians did; he aimed at a natural look and rhythm of speech, then exaggerated it just enough to mine the humor in a character.

A great mimic of voice and gesture, Mogulesco could impersonate anyone: rich, poor, male, female, elder, youth. A memoirist of the period recalled "a gnarled old lady on the stage, who looked as if she had wandered in from the street. The action took place on a ship bound for America. She had to be vaccinated and put out her skinny trembling arm; her whole body quivered; every wrinkle in her bewildered face fluttered. The curtain fell. The audience cheered 'Mogulesco.' The old woman appeared, smiled charmingly, bowed and left. Afterward I went backstage and met Mogulesco, slim and elegant, a sensitive cheerful face, not a sign of the exhausted crone."

Oddly enough, while Mogulesco began the elevation of the crowd, it was the ebullient, unsubtle Thomashefsky who brought it to another plane. In 1889, Boris held forth at the Thalia, a 3,000-seat theater at 46–48 Bowery; Jacob Adler performed across the street, at the 3,500-seat Windsor, 45–47 Bowery. To counteract the commercially successful operettas, Adler made a curtain call one evening to announce that he would open as Othello to Kessler's Iago. On alternate nights the two would switch roles. The role of the Moor, he added with a withering reference to Thomashefsky, was no mere "Princeling of Jerusalem." This was a part that demanded a *real* actor, a specialist.

Boris rose to the bait, advertised his coming appearance in *Hamlet*, commissioned a translation, and starred in it, as promised. And his production turned out to be the more successful. The Thomashefsky Prince of Denmark played to standees. (Actually, he could have recited the front page of Hearst's *American* and filled the house with young women. One evening an enthusiast actually started to strip in the aisle and was shown the door.) At the conclusion of *Hamlet*, calls of "Author! Author!" resounded almost every night. Boris didn't have the heart to say that "Shekspir," as the audience called him, had been dead for almost three hundred years. A trouper volunteered to go out, claim authorship, and acknowledge the approbation, but instead, according to Bessie Thomashefsky, "We just used to ask them to forgive us, but Shakespeare lived far away in England, and could not come to see his play."

Nonetheless Moishe was rapidly maturing; the bardic presentations had deepened the hunger for serious, demanding theater. In 1903, Lower East Side patrons witnessed the cheeky, breakthrough performance of Bertha Kalisch. Along with the actresses Sarah Adler, Jacob's third wife, and Bessie Thomashefsky, Boris's long-suffering but only spouse, Kalisch dominated the Yiddish theater. The beautiful young woman had appeared in Goldfaden's early productions, but even the father of Yiddish theater could not hold her for long.

In 1896, at twenty-four, she came to America and immediately picked up roles at the Thalia. Four years later, Bertha Kalisch's name sat atop Bowery marquees, and unlike Bessie and Sarah, she had climbed there without the benefit of an impresario husband. Now she dared to follow the lead of Sarah Bernhardt.

The year before, the Divine Sarah had brought her notorious production of *Hamlet* to England, with herself in the title role. Encouraged by backers and fans, Kalisch was next to cross the gender line. Her performance won surprisingly favorable notices not only from the Yiddish papers but also from outside the ghetto. The critic for the *New York Morning Journal* happily reported, "There were no airs, there were no frills. There were no poses, no struggles for elusive effect." The female star "got down to the solid bedrock of the idea and hammered at it." As Joel Berkowitz notes in his luminous study *Shakespeare on the American Yiddish Stage*, Bertha Kalisch's *Hamlet* "was no mere drawing-room experiment. It was popular theater—popular enough not only to remain in her repertoire as long as she remained in the Yiddish theater, but also to appeal to the 'uptown' critics."

Those reviewers would come downtown the same year to see the most significant portrayal in Yiddish theater history. On reflection, Jacob Adler said that he derived enormous pleasure from playing "simple Jews, Jews who were clowns, fools, *shlimazls*, unfortunates." But these characters were mere walk-ons, cameos compared with "the Jew of high intellect, proud convictions, and grand character." That personage was the Shylock of Shakespeare's *Merchant of Venice*. The Adler version, presented at the People's Theater a few months after the Kalisch splash, had an unusual aspect: a Jewish actor was playing the stage's most infamous Jew.

Adler refused to follow the lead of Henry Irving. The English actor had made the Venetian moneylender a resolute gentleman, obliged to defend himself against Christian malice. This radical and sympathetic interpretation had enjoyed a warm reception in the late 1800s; but Adler, who had seen Irving's striking performance in London, wanted no part of it. He saw in Shylock "a patriarch, a higher being. A certain grandeur, the triumph of long patience, intellect, and character has been imparted to him by his teachers: suffering and tradition."

In order to give Shylock "the prominence he deserved," Adler ruthlessly edited *The Merchant of Venice*, excising scenes he thought unnecessary and altering the text so that his character remained onstage more than half the time. En route, he commissioned musical accompaniments by Joseph Rumshinsky. The composer knew the actor professionally. He got a more intimate view of Adler's character one evening when the two men strolled past a Yiddish theater. It housed one of Adler's favorite plays, but a lesser celebrity now had the role. In reminiscence, Rumshinsky wrote, "I wanted to take Jacob to the stage door, but he ran in to the lobby. By this time I was convinced he was insane."

Rumshinsky continued, "Adler ran down the aisle, stopped in the middle, and shouted in Yiddish, 'I am here, I am with you! We'll play for you, we'll give you good theater!'" The curtain rang down in the middle of the scene. Hustling to a dressing room, Adler began to apply makeup. "He said to me, 'Rumshinsky, my friend, I love theater! But I'm only onstage two or three hours a day, so I have to turn the rest of my life into theater!'

"When he was ready, the curtain rose and the play started again, from the beginning."

Still, just as the excitable Adler could persuade women into bed, he could also get artists to do his bidding. Rumshinsky created some of his best work for this new production. The theme he provided for Shylock was a grave, haunting cello solo, in contrast to a buoyant, fully orchestrated melody for the capricious Venetians. Aided by the mood music, Adler redefined Shakespeare's problematical Jew in two pivotal scenes. The first was the shattering discovery that Shylock's daughter, Jessica, had eloped with Lorenzo, a Christian. In the Irving production, Shylock knocked at the door of the enemy's house three times, each time a little louder, with increasing desperation as the curtain came down. Irving's contemporary Sir Herbert Beerbohm Tree played the same scene more explicitly, pacing across the stage, crying out in sorrow and covering his head with ashes.

Adler took it a step further. He opened the front door with an immense key and entered silently. After an almost unbearable pause, he spoke his daughter's name. Silence. He spoke it again, the voice hopelessly booming out "Jessicaaaaaa!" and echoing in a vast and empty room. He came out, bowed down with sorrow, to settle on a bench, his voice quavering with a barely audible Yiddish lament. As the curtain fell, he slowly tore his garment—a sign of mourning for the child who has left the faith and whom he must now regard as dead.

In the last scene, the court's verdict goes against Shylock: he must forsake his gold and convert to Christianity. His enemy Gratiano sneers, "In christening shalt thou have two godfathers. Had I been judge, thou shouldst have had ten more, to bring thee to the gallows, not the font." In all the other productions, Gratiano pushed Shylock to the ground where he sat, whimpering and defeated, the old Hebrew *in extremis*, victim of his own avarice. In the Adler version, Shylock was also forced to earth, but after a few moments he rose up. From his garment he brushed the dirt of the floor and, symbolically, the filth of bias. With an air of moral superiority and innate dignity, he made his exit. "Weighty and proud his walk," the star recalled, "calm and conclusive his speech, a man of rich personal and national experience, a man who sees life through the glasses of eternity. So I played him, so I had joy in him, and so I portrayed him."

The portrait of Shylock electrified the Lower East Side, as intended. What Adler could not have predicted was the clamor outside the little world of the Yiddish theater. The mainstream press embraced the production. Invoking the great eighteenth-century English actor/impresario, *Theater* magazine dubbed Jacob "The Bowery Garrick," and the prominent producer Arthur Hopkins came downtown to make an unprecedented offer. He wanted to present the Adler Shylock on Broadway—not entirely in Yiddish; after all, Hopkins had to keep a wide, largely Gentile audience in mind. But the interpretation, the movements would be identical to those at the People's, and the focus would remain on the Yiddish-speaking moneylender. The rest of the cast would recite their lines in English.

However bizarre—an unstable amalgam of art and promotion—Hopkins's offer seemed too flattering to refuse. Adler signed the contract. He first tried out his Shylock in Boston and Washington, where patronizing critics spoke of it as a novelty rather than a breakthrough. Never mind, Hopkins assured his cast; New York would be different.

And so it proved. *The Merchant of Venice* opened at the American Theater on May 24, 1903, and rave notices showered down. ADLER SCORES IN SHYLOCK ROLE trumpeted a headline in the *Herald*, and the article went on to call Jacob's version "that rare dramatic experience on Broadway, the coincidence of a great play and a great actor." The *Evening Journal* enthused that Adler "played the character in a way never seen on the American stage and defying imitation." The performance revealed Shylock "as the Jew of the ages." In the judgment of *Theater* magazine, the Jewish actor offered "a striking and original conception, wrought out not only of careful study, but above all from a racial sympathy, an instinctive appreciation of the deeper motives of this profound and complex character."

No surprise that the Jewish press would *kvell* as one of its own received such glowing notices. But what was surprising was that most of the reviews paid more attention to the ticket buyers than to the actor. The *Yiddish World*, for example, found "a deep seriousness on the faces of these Americans. They understood Adler just as well as they did the rest of the actors, and in places even better. They showed this with both the attentiveness and the applause with which they greeted the end of every scene in which he appeared."

Adler became the darling of the establishment press and of his Broadway peers. Steffens encouraged his readers to take the subway down to the Lower East Side. Even if they couldn't understand a word, he wrote, they would apprehend the gestures and the themes of "the best theater in New York." The establishment critics George Jean Nathan and Stark Young dropped by Adler's dressing room; so did matinee idol John Drew. In the days to follow, the spirit of the ghetto took a galvanic leap. What the public schools taught the ghetto's children was demonstrably true: humble beginnings were no bar to achievement in America. Old hands and greenhorns endlessly discussed this truth in cafés, social clubs, and sweatshops. A Yiddish proverb made the rounds: *Men ken makhn dem kholem gresser vi di nakht*: One can blow up a dream to be bigger than the night. Given the spectacular rise of Jacob Adler, who could disagree?

In fact Adler never went back to Broadway. Having made his point, he contentedly stayed on Second Avenue for the rest of his career. But after the Shylock triumph, Yiddish theater would never be the same. The works of Hurwitz and Lateiner became unfashionable, and when Abraham Goldfaden immigrated to the Lower East Side in 1907 he found himself a back number, outdistanced by his offspring. No one had any interest in his old plays. When he wrote a new one, *Ben Ami*, about a false messiah, one producer bought it out of charity; at a reading, the actors openly mocked the dialogue. The old man overheard one performer refer to him as senile. Goldfaden left the room shocked and demoralized. From then on, he kept asking his wife and his few friends whether he had lost his senses. Out of pity, Jacob Adler sent Goldfaden five dollars a week so that he could eat and pay the rent for his meager flat, and Thomashefsky took an option on *Ben Ami*, motivated by guilt and sorrow.

And then a miracle happened. At a second reading, the actors proved excited by the prospect of putting on a retro melodrama. Gratefully, Goldfaden told Thomashefsky that he lived now for a chance at vindication before the Yiddish-speaking public. He would be content with one last success—a coda to his life in art. Then, he proclaimed, he could die happy.

Ben Ami opened on Christmas Day 1907 to an avid response. The rest of the story could have been part of a Goldfaden *mise-en-scène*. There were curtain calls, a speech, flowers. The old playwright walked down Second Avenue accompanied by his admirers. Just before he reached his doorstep, they placed a garland around his neck. He walked into the apartment and greeted his wife, weeping: "They gave me laurel wreaths. I'm not senile, I'm not senile!" For the next five nights he sat in a box watching performances of his play. On the sixth evening he felt feverish, left before the final curtain, and died in his sleep that night.

A funeral procession some thirty thousand strong made its way from the ghetto to Washington Cemetery in Brooklyn. Many offered valedictories; Thomashefsky's over-the-top oration put them all in the shade. "If not for our old father Goldfaden," he intoned, "we none of us would have become tragedians or comedians, prima donnas, soubrettes, playwrights. If not for Goldfaden, we'd be plain and simple Jews: cantors, choir singers, folk singers, clowns, clothes peddlers, machine sewers, cigarette makers, Purim players, wedding jugglers, clothes pressers and finishers." He paused for breath and went on: "Goldfaden went out like a light in his dark room while we, his children, ride in carriages, own our own houses, are hung with diamonds. Union members, club members, pinochle players, decision makers, managers, sports. We're nice and warm, all of us. But our father was cold."

Ben Ami ran for months, just as Goldfaden had dreamed. But that production became the coda for the old-style Yiddish theater. Fed up with light fare, audiences now demanded substance. Kessler got his wish; no longer did he have to dress up like a turkey. An advertisement in the Yiddish-language *Forward* listed him in adaptations of Tolstoy's *Kreutzer Sonata* as well as in four contemporary dramas—all in a single week.

By then, a new generation of writers had broken through.

Jacob Gordin, who began as a journalist, stressed realism over fantasy. In his debut, *Siberia*, a man finds himself condemned to prison for a misdemeanor. En route north he slips his chains, rejoins his family, changes his name, and assumes another way of life. He prospers and becomes a respectable leader in his community. A rival, jealous of the man's success, discovers his secret and informs the police. Arrest and martyrdom follow.

The Lower East Siders had never encountered an original Yiddish play like this—no jokes, no promise of hope or reconciliation, no songs, and none of the big, ornamented speeches that ghetto dwellers adored. Yet audiences flocked to see Gordin's terse presentation of sorrow and rue. His domestic drama, *Wild Man*, was even more popular. This strange prefiguring of Faulkner starred Jacob Adler in the title role. The plot was simple, the effect overpowering. A feebleminded youth falls in love with his stepmother without understanding his strange new emotions. "The poor fellow," wrote Hapgood, "is filled with the mysterious wonderings of an incapable mind. His shadow terrifies and interests him. He is puzzled and worried by everything; the slightest sound terrifies him. The burlesque which Mr. Adler puts into the part was inserted to please the crowd, but increases the horror of it, as when Lear went mad; for the Elizabethan audiences laughed, and had their souls wrung at the same time."

Leon Kobrin, a Gordin disciple, originally preferred to write in his native Russian: Yiddish was more appropriate to tell "simple tales for servant girls and ignoramuses." But he soon succumbed to the culture of the tenements and to the spell of the theater. Yiddish play after Yiddish play tumbled from his pen, most of them about contemporary people and current dilemmas. The titles are eloquent: *The East Side Ghetto*; *Minna, or the Ruined Family from Downtown*; *Sonia from East Broadway*.

As for Sholem Asch, nothing seemed beyond his talent. His plays reached far beyond the ghetto, to seventeenth-century pogroms, Jewish criminals, the garment industry, Christian history. "I am not a Jewish artist," he insisted, even though he continued to write in Yiddish. "I am a universal artist." Few disagreed. His plays drew audiences all over the world. In the same vein, *The Treasure*, a play about a shtetl transfixed by the rumor of money buried in a local graveyard, was written by one of the most Americanized of the new writers, Russian-born Columbia grad David Pinski. It became a Lower East Side hit after famed director Max Reinhardt first staged the work in Germany in 1910. Harvard professor George Pierce Baker, teacher of Eugene O'Neill, George Abbott, and other Broadway luminaries, read *The Treasure* in translation and compared Pinski to Ben Jonson. If the Yiddish playwright's dialogue "lacks the poetic expression of *Volpone*," Baker wrote, "it has a finer truth of characterization."

Following the Great War, the old guard slowly relinquished its hold. One evening in 1920, David Kessler suffered abdominal pains. He went on anyway, and then collapsed; rushed to the hospital, he died during emergency surgery. Jacob Adler's health failed in the early 1920s. He made his last bow in Gordin's *The Stranger* in 1924. Struggling to remember his lines at the Second Avenue Theater, he hobbled across the stage on a cane, and then received eighteen curtain calls from a weeping audience. In his dressing room, Adler's wife exclaimed, "You made them cry as never before."

Yes, he acknowledged with a few tears of his own. "But it was not my art that made them cry." Shortly afterward, Thomashefsky tried to bring Yiddish theater to Broadway, to no avail, and his career fell into a long tailspin.

By then, other troupes had pushed their way onstage. A young actor-director, Jacob Ben-Ami, took the limelight, emphasizing the new "intensive reality" of theorist Konstantin Stanislavsky. Ben-Ami's innovations freed the Yiddish stage from the forehead-smiting, breast-beating style adopted by too many of the lesser players and began yet another renaissance on Second Avenue. Appraising the downtown scene in the early 1930s, *Theater* magazine enthused, "The Yiddish theater is now superior to the American. Yiddish theater is aimed at art."

Equally up to date, almost every member of the sensational Artef (a Yiddish acronym for Worker's Theater Group) was a hard-line Communist. Predictably, the Artef's work was symbolic and stark, emphasizing the group rather than the individual. Productions were revolutionary in more than the political sense, with dazzling set designs and acting that displayed a polish and discipline that other performers secretly envied. Jealous competitors were quick to mock the troupe's mannerisms. Maurice Schwartz jeered at radical performers who made "peculiar motions with their hands, speaking in squeaky tones, rolling their eyes, sighing at the moon." They spoke "the way people are going to speak in the future, millions of years from now . . . everything the reverse of natural; pointed walls and furniture, holding a walking stick upside down, jumping instead of walking, and instead of natural human faces—backwards noses and crooked cheeks."

Other groups stayed away from politics and flourished. Yiddish films came out, including Gordin's *Mirele Efros*, a kind of updated "Queen Lear," and *Tevye the Dairyman*—progenitor of *Fiddler on the Roof*—starring Maurice Schwartz in the title role. Two of Jacob Adler's daughters, Celia and Stella, became Yiddish theater stars; his son, Luther, was the original *Golden Boy* in Clifford Odets's Broadway drama and soon made a name in Hollywood. Josef Buloff and Joseph Schildkraut appeared in American movies. So, even more spectacularly, did Meshilem Weisenfreund, the son of Yiddish theater producers, who, at twelve, went on in an emergency to play the small part of a doddering ancient and who, renamed Paul Muni, received five Academy Award nominations and won an Oscar for his starring role in the *The Story of Louis Pasteur*.

As Muni rose, however, the Yiddish theater seemed to experience an equal and opposite reaction. By the late 1930s the Lower East Side's Jewish population began to disperse to the outer boroughs, to better digs uptown, or to the burgeoning suburbs. Only a few signs of life remained. WEVD ("the station that speaks your language") continued to entertain listeners with plays and interviews in Yiddish. Molly Picon's winsome personality and Menashe Skulnik's unabashed clowning found welcome not only on the Yiddish stage but on television and in movies. Ben Bonus founded a Yiddish theater in Hollywood and toured America with his wife, Mina Bern.

The charismatic Maurice Schwartz, fluent enough to pursue a career uptown or in films, stayed in his Yiddish Art Theater on Twelfth Street and Second Avenue. Under his aegis the troupe staged experimental "Grotesque-Cubist" productions of works like *The Dybbuk* as well as new translations of Gorky, Schnitzler, Shaw, Molière, Chekhov, and Shakespeare. Occasionally Schwartz could out-Ziegfeld Ziegfeld. His version of Sholem Asch's spectacular *Sanctification of the Name*, for example, boasted forty-two speaking roles, crowd scenes with fifty supernumeraries, ornate sets, orchestral music, choreography, and a fifty-six-page program. Audiences, at first jarred, soon realized they were in the presence of a new and modern sensibility. Uptown critic John Mason Brown, astonished, raved about a "vast energy, a blatant, exciting kind of underscoring that is more familiar to Berlin than to Broadway." *New York Times* drama reviewer Brooks Atkinson agreed: whenever you see this unique performer, he wrote, "you know you are not in a library."

But Schwartz turned out to be the last superstar. One by one the Yiddish venues folded, as did the newspapers that had reviewed and discussed so much *shund* and classic drama. Alas, the one king no Yiddish actor could impersonate was Canute, and the tide of assimilation flowed on. As the next generation of Jews caught on in New York, entering the professions, writing (with unconscious irony) Ph.D. dissertations on Henry James, and establishing themselves in business and in show business, Yiddish became a discomfiting singsong antique, a reminder of teeming slums and greenhorn culture. When the Yiddish marquee names passed on, no one replaced them.

All too soon the Hebrew Actors Union on Seventh Street, a powerhouse guild from the early 1920s to the 1950s, became a meetinghouse for retirees who sat on hard chairs, smoked, and reminisced about better times. The late Seymour Rexite, a union president, once spoke to me about the men and women he had watched and learned from and acted with a world ago. Around his neck he wore a gold Magen David. "They call this the Star of David," he said. "Well, this is only one star. I worked with hundreds of stars of David, Jewish stars who outshone the streetlights, the stage lights, the sun, sometimes." But today, he sadly observed, the only place you could find young players of Yiddish was the Folksbiene Theater. Almost alone, that group was (and still is) dedicated to keeping the flame alive, sometimes using supertitles because so few audience members can understand the *mamaloshen*.

In *World of Our Fathers*, Irving Howe offers a valedictory. In order for the Yiddish theater to have survived, he argues, "some sort of leap was necessary, as Schwartz's Art Theater and the Artef at their best undertook, from folk to cosmopolitan." But this could happen "only if there had been more time, only if there had been several generations that used Yiddish as their native tongue yet were also at home in Western culture." The rush to assimilate put paid to that: "It was a theater blazing with the eloquence of its moment, and in the memories of a few the glow would remain."

Well, if the Yiddish theater itself has vanished, its glow is more than metaphoric. The fervor, the cultural ambition, the pure chutzpah animated a generation of showfolk who followed the giants. Lee Strasberg, a founder of the Actors Studio, never forgot his introduction to the world of performance when, as a child, he watched David Kessler—"clearly an actor of great temperament." Stella Adler, Jacob's daughter, became another of the most prominent acting teachers in the world. Concerning the audience, she wrote, "I have a mission right from the old man, who said, 'Make it better for them. Otherwise, why are they here?'" Her mission quite literally covered the *Waterfront*. The star of that film acknowledged his debt not long ago. "If there wasn't the Yiddish theater," observed Marlon Brando, "there wouldn't have been Stella. And if there hadn't been Stella, there wouldn't have been all these actors who studied with her and changed the face of theater—and not only acting, but directing and writing."

Indeed, stage and film directors from Harold Clurman to Sidney Lumet pursued directing careers because of what they saw early on in the Yiddish theater. And the pupils of Adler and Strasberg and their colleagues form a pantheon of American performance. In addition to Brando, exemplars include Montgomery Clift, Paul Newman, Martin Landau, Meryl Streep, Dustin Hoffman, Jack Nicholson, Robert De Niro, Al Pacino, and Ellen Burstyn. Brian De Palma's remake of *Scarface*, one of the most popular DVD rentals for the last several years, bases itself on Paul Muni's 1932 feature. Recalls Pacino, who played the title role: "The film just stopped me in my tracks. All I wanted to do was imitate the central character. The acting went beyond the boundaries of naturalism into another kind of expression. It was almost abstract what he did. It was almost uplifting."

This "other kind of expression"—authentic, concentrated, persuasive—was the true spirit of the Yiddish theater. It animated the professionals who acted on its stages, and they in turn breathed it into their colleagues on Broadway and in Hollywood. The phrases of the Yiddish theater are no longer in the original tongue, but the fervor, the intensity, and the chutzpah persist, now part of the deepest essence of American drama.

The Dynamo and the Jeweler

Jacob was a delinquent in the making. The twelve-year-old had no use for school; the street was his academy, and roller skating and fighting his favorite subjects. His older brother, Israel, was another story: quiet, intellectual, in love with words and ideas. Understandably, their parents, Morris and Rose Gershowitz, acquired an upright with the older boy in mind. But the law of unintended consequences applied in 1910 as in any century. When Jacob sat down at the keyboard, he fluently rattled off a few popular numbers, with dazzling left-handed embellishments. As it turned out, the boy had been practicing, playing by ear on a neighbor's piano.

By then the Gershowitzes had streamlined the family name to Gershwin and Americanized the boys' monikers to George and Ira. In this, and in many other ways, they were no different from a lot of immigrant Russian Jews during the early twentieth century: vigorous, close-knit, eager to get on in the Promised City. Morris led the way. "My father," Ira recalled, "engaged in various activities: restaurants, Russian and Turkish baths, bakeries, a cigar store and pool parlor on the 42nd Street side of what is now Grand Central

Station, bookmaking at the Brighton Beach racetrack for three exciting but disastrous weeks."

The paterfamilias preferred to be within walking distance of his various enterprises, which meant changing residences every year or so, shuttling from the Lower East Side to midtown to Brooklyn and then back again to Manhattan—some thirty locations in all, as the family fortunes swung freely from middle-class comfort to near-bankruptcy and back again. The Gershwins' two younger children, Arthur and Frances, came along during flush times, receiving closer attention and better educations than their elder siblings. In the early years, Morris's ventures absorbed at least sixteen hours of his day, leaving George and Ira to fend for themselves in a city full of temptations.

Ira was saved by shelves of schoolbooks, George by eighty-eight keys. "Studying the piano made a good boy out of a bad one," George once reflected. "I was a changed person after I took it up." A procession of teachers taught him to read music and opened his ears with Chopin, Debussy, and Liszt. By the time Charles Hambitzer entered the scene, George was experimenting with a few pieces of his own, more original than the part-time conductor and composer had ever encountered. In a letter he prophesied: "I have a pupil who will make his mark in music if anybody will. The boy is a genius, without a doubt; he's just crazy about music and can't wait until it's time to take his lesson. . . . He wants to go in for this modern stuff, jazz and what not. But I'm not going to let him for a while. I'll see that he gets a firm foundation in the classics first."

George paid close attention to his teacher for almost two years, but the modern stuff proved irresistible. At fifteen, he dropped out of the High School of Commerce and played himself into a job as pianist at Jerome H. Remick and Company, publishers of popular songs. He demonstrated new music in stores around the city, checked vaudeville houses to make sure that Remick songs were performed, and plugged a few of his own melodies. The pianist came to understand what the public loved and what it rejected out of hand. Isaac Goldberg, George's earliest biographer, noted that audiences "wanted snap and 'pep'; pep, indeed, was just beginning to come into our vocabulary, and by the same token, into our life. And pep was part of George's nature. He had been made for the new day."

Irving Berlin, then America's hottest songwriter, heard George at the keyboard one afternoon. The young man's sense of harmony instantly impressed him, as did his ability to write tunes that jumped directly into the listener's brain. On the spot, Berlin offered Gershwin a job as his musical secretary—and then, on second thought, withdrew it. "You're more than the skilled arranger I'm looking for," he said. "You're a natural-born creator. This sort of job would cramp you. You're meant for big things."

Word of this meeting circulated in the old neighborhood. Boris Thomashefsky, the Yiddish theater's most commercial actor/impresario, summoned George to his Second Avenue dressing room, along with Sholom Secunda, composer of the international hit "Bei Mir Bist Du Schoen." Boris thought they could collaborate on a series of operettas. Each man played a few of his own tunes on the rehearsal piano. Before George hit his stride, Sholom shook his head. "The two of us are no pair," he said. "We have totally different approaches in music." Afterward, whenever the musicians met, George would pump Sholom's hand delightedly and tell anyone within listening distance, "If he had agreed to become my partner, I would now be a composer in the Yiddish theater."

Meantime Ira, on his own track, was graduating from high school, reading a book a week, working odd jobs, and attending City College classes with his boyhood pal E. Y. "Yip" Harburg (later Harold Arlen's lyricist for *The Wizard of Oz*). The two young men tried out light verse in an undergraduate publication, writing on equal terms, until Yip announced that his favorite book of poetry was W. S. Gilbert's *Bab Ballads.* Ira informed him that the rhymes were only 50 percent of the story; music accompanied those words. This was news to Yip, who got an invite to the Gershwins' home to hear the score of *H.M.S. Pinafore* on their Victrola. "There were all the lines I knew by heart," Harburg later wrote. "I was dumbfounded, staggered!"

Ira yearned to play Gilbert to his brother's Sullivan. The trouble was, a young lyricist named Irving Caesar had already taken the position. Irving and George enjoyed working together; they turned out one catchy song in just fifteen minutes. A few months later the composer contrived to get an invitation to a party attended by Al Jolson, the most popular entertainer of the day. Gershwin worked his way to the piano and performed his and Irving's "Swanee." Jolson loved the song so much he interpolated it into his already-running Broadway show, *Sinbad.* In 1919 the phonograph record sold more than two million copies; you could find the sheet music in almost every parlor in the nation. George wrote several more songs with Caesar—though none as popular as "Swanee"—and then teamed with B. G. De Sylva for a series of light *Ziegfeld Follies*–style Broadway revues called *George White's Scandals.*

The third year of the Gershwin/De Sylva collaboration produced a breakthrough piece, *Blue Monday*, in which George gave notice that he was no longer content in Tin Pan Alley. He intended to be nothing less than the bridge between American popular music and classical music. Wrote biographer Goldberg, "It was the hey-day of the new jazz, and Gotham was in the midst of a concurrent Negrophilia." Gershwin seized the moment and composed a one-act opera based on American themes. Set in a Harlem barroom, *Blue Monday* concerned a couple whose romance ended in violence. Reviewers dismissed the simplistic plot, but most found the music beguiling. The *New York Sun* critic had an especially clear crystal ball: "Here at last is a genuinely human plot of American life, set to music in the popular vein, using jazz only at the right moments, the sentimental song, the Blues, and above all, a new and free ragtime recitative. True, there were crudities, but in it we see the first gleam of a new American musical art."

But George was still a songwriter first and a serious composer second. Even while he worked with other lyricists, he brought in his brother for occasional "singles," offering them to vaudeville and Broadway headliners. One, "The Real American Folk Song," was the first all-Gershwin number to say something about the country and its new music:

The real American folk song is a rag—
A mental jag—
A rhythmic tonic for the chronic blues,
The critics called it a joke song, but now
They've changed their tune
And they like it somehow.
For it's inoculated
With a syncopated
Sort of meter,
Sweeter
Than a classic strain . . .
The real American folk song—
A master stroke song—
IS A RAG!

The key to that song is the word "syncopated," indicating emphases on the unexpected beats. Traditional music, classic and pop, relies on a standard rhythm: four-four time, for example, would count off *one*, two, three, four. Syncopation, in contrast, would be one *two*, three *four*—a refreshment for the ear but hell for the lyricist, especially an exacting one like Ira, who soon became known by his sobriquet: the Jeweler.

Pop diva Nora Bayes agreed to sing "Folk Song" in her revue, *Ladies First*, at the Broadhurst Theater. It was the first time Ira had ever heard one of his works performed for an audience, and he hungered for more applause.

But the brothers still had a way to go before their paths truly converged. Now that Ira had proved himself in the theater, he found himself collaborating with Vincent Youmans on a couple of undistinguished shows while George established his reputation with half a dozen Broadway smashes, working with Caesar, De Sylva, and other wordsmiths.

Then, in 1921, the famous brother persuaded a producer to let him write with an unknown talent named Arthur Francis. George described the lyricist as "a college kid with loads of talent." The kid, of course, was Ira, who had concocted his pseudonym from the first names of his younger siblings. The team provided a study in contrasts; it was hard to believe they shared the same parents. George was a dynamo—handsome, agile, mercurial, a smoker and chewer of cigars. Energy seemed to radiate from his fingers and eyes. A Gershwin number described him perfectly: "Oh, I Can't Sit Down!" Ira was a worrier—pudgy, contemplative, a pipe-smoking personification of another Gershwin song: "I Won't Say I Will, I Won't Say I Won't."

Their first musical, *A Dangerous Maid*, enjoyed modest success in 1921; so did *For Goodness Sake* in 1922. Neither production featured any hits; that sort of triumph would wait another two years. By then, George had established himself as America's first crossover musician, linking the raucous nightclub and the decorous concert hall in something he called *Rhapsody in Blue*. Conductor Paul Whiteman remembered the audience at Aeolian Hall on the epochal afternoon of February 12, 1924. In addition to Sergei Rachmaninoff, Victor Herbert, and Jascha Heifetz, it included "vaudevillians, concert managers come to have a look at the novelty, Tin Pan Alleyites, opera stars, flappers, all mixed up higgledy-piggledy." That motley group reflected Gershwin's rhapsody, played by the composer himself. From the first clarinet glissando to the fluent chords in the middle to the broad melodic finale, *Rhapsody in Blue* enthralled the audience. All of *haute* New York seemed caught in the skeins of George's music. It suggested the rhythms of black jazz, the melancholy strains of Yiddish folk melodies, the kinetic force of Manhattan in the Speakeasy Era, as well as the art of the Old Masters.

The crowd went wild, and even though a few critics carped at the composer's use of "colored jazz music," most were intrigued. The *New York Herald* critic was typical: "Mr. Gershwin will be heard from often, and one music lover earnestly hopes that he will keep to the field in which he is a free and independent creator, and not permit himself to be led away into the academic groves and buried in the shadows of ancient trees."

Not a chance. By the time the buzz died down, the twenty-five-year-old was already at work on a new show with his brother. During the composition of *Lady Be Good*, produced in 1924, Arthur Francis disappeared. For the first time a musical unabashedly presented itself as the work of George and Ira Gershwin. It starred two former vaudevillians, Fred and Adele Astaire, and contained bursts of poetry and melody that would enter the American repertoire, including the title number, "The Man I Love," and "Fascinating Rhythm." George had admired Fred's work since his vaudeville days; after watching one routine backstage he asked, "Wouldn't it be great if I could write a musical show and you could be in it?" Well, now George had written one, and Fred and his sister were its leads. Everyone who saw *Lady* knew they were at the beginning of something special—the confluence of the Astaires and the Gershwins. In the next decade Adele would retire, but Fred would carry on. With a new partner he would lead George and Ira far up on the stairway to paradise.

Even in the Roaring Twenties the Gershwins had a few detractors, but critics had never meant much to George. It was Ira who took them seriously, forever revising his verse, aiming for a Platonic ideal that he never quite achieved. After Ira's emergence as a major lyricist, almost all his colleagues wrote salutes to the man's industry and exactitude. But there is a notable exception. In an ungenerous (and inaccurate) assessment, Stephen Sondheim commented, "It's rare in an Ira Gershwin lyric where you don't feel the sweat because he's shoving so many rhymes in." By contrast, *My Fair Lady* lyricist Alan Jay Lerner, who knew a thing or two about rhyme and rhythm, wrote that he was "overwhelmed by the wonderfully slangy sentimentality and ingenious versatility of Ira." Lerner's was the people's voice, too. For every Sondheim phrase that has worked its way into the common language—"send in the clowns," say—Ira Gershwin could easily provide ten: "lady be good," "nice work if you can get it," "our love is here to stay," "stairway to paradise," "someone to watch over me," "'s wonderful," "how long has this been going on?," "I got rhythm," "it ain't necessarily so," "they can't take that away from me," to name a few.

Moreover, unlike Cole Porter, Noel Coward, or, for that matter, Sondheim himself, Ira seldom had the luxury of writing music to accommodate his words. George's music came first, the headlong tempi demonstrating the composer's pep—today it would be called gusto on steroids. The speed of "Fascinating Rhythm," for example, made Ira hurry his verse:

Fascinating Rhythm
You've got me on the go!
Fascinating Rhythm
I'm all a-quiver!

What a mess you're making!
The neighbors want to know
Why I'm always shaking
Just like a flivver.

By the time of *Oh, Kay!* in 1926, though, George had learned to write for onstage characters. His yearning, blues-tinted melodies now began to mark the second Gershwin style, one that concerned itself with emotion *and* tempo. "Someone to Watch Over Me" is typical of this period, George using a poignant, drawn-out theme, Ira matching him with the tangy assertions of a Jazz Age dreamer:

Although he may not be the man some
Girls think of as handsome,
To my heart he'll carry the key.

Won't you tell him, please,
To put on some speed,
Follow my lead?
Oh, how I need
Someone to watch over me.

Gilbert Seldes, the first American critic to take the popular arts seriously, worried that George might be going effete and highbrow with his serious concert music. In *Esquire* Seldes grumbled: "It is as if Gershwin were writing for the five thousand people who go to the Lido, know the best club in London, can't count above 21 in New York, and depend on [society hostess] Elsa Maxwell for a good time."

But *Oh, Kay!* put these fears to rest. Gertrude Lawrence sang the lead number, and, as the composer recalled, she had the stage to herself. "It was all very wistful, and, on opening night, somewhat to the surprise of the management, Miss Lawrence sang the song to a doll. This doll was a strange-looking object I found in a Philadelphia toy store and gave to her with the suggestion that she use it in the number. The doll stayed in the show for the entire run."

Just as George's affecting new music and fascinating rhythms became his signature, the argot of the times became Ira's ID. In *Funny Face* he stood Broadway on its ear by fracturing the word "it's" into pieces, using only the last consonant:

'S wonderful! 'S marvelous—
You should care for me!
'S awful nice! 'S Paradise—
'S what I love to see!
My dear, it's four-leaf-clover time
From now on my heart's working overtime.

And in "How Long Has This Been Going On?" he turned an exclamation into the personification of a beautiful girl:

I could cry salty tears;
Where have I been all these years?
Little wow,
Tell me now:
How long has this been going on?

With royalties pouring in, George and Ira moved their parents and siblings to a large West Side apartment. Ira courted and wed

Lenore Strunsky, but the marriage barely interrupted the brothers' collaboration. In 1929 they rented adjoining penthouses at 33 Riverside Drive, where Ira was usually content to stay at home fussing over nuances and phrases while George was always happy to attend a party, provided his host had a grand piano on which he could regale the guests with a medley of his melodies played *con brio*. When not committed to a show, George traveled to London and the Continent, searching out conductors and composers. Introduced to Maurice Ravel in Paris, he expressed a wish to study with the maestro. Replied Ravel, "But I was coming to America to study with you." A probably apocryphal version of the story has George asking Stravinsky for lessons, with the Russian, mindful of the successful Gershwin's huge income, responding, "How about you give *me* some lessons?"

At about this time, recalled playwright S. N. Behrman, George "was becoming one of the most eligible bachelors in America; there was curiosity among his friends from the beginning as to who the girl would be." There had been brief liaisons with starlets, a long-term romance with composer Kay Swift, and a serious fling with a "physical culture" teacher, whom George called the Dream Girl. In the midst of that last romance, Behrman received a call from Ira with "some devastating news. He hadn't the heart to tell George. He begged me to relieve him of this disagreeable chore. I took on the job. I went up to George's room; he was working on the *Concerto in F*. He played me a passage; he completed a variation on it.

"'George,' I said, 'I have bad news for you. Dream Girl is married.' His brown eyes showed a flicker of pain. He kept looking at me. Finally, he spoke. 'Do you know?' he said, 'If I weren't so busy, I'd feel terrible.'"

The *Concerto*, debuting at Carnegie Hall, showed that *Rhapsody in Blue* was no fluke. George had no intention of abandoning his first love, the Broadway stage, but the ambitious composer never lost sight of his second love, the concert stage. Just when he began thinking of another, longer piece, though, a third love came along—the sound stage. Hollywood beckoned, and George and Ira went west. Their first film, *Delicious*, appeared in 1931 as the depression settled over the land. The score was unremarkable; the movie bombed.

Other teams might have wallowed in sunshine and self-pity. The Gershwins packed up, returned to Broadway—and won the Pulitzer Prize. When George S. Kaufman observed, "Satire is something that closes on Saturday night," he obviously forgot the book he had confected for *Of Thee I Sing*, a hilarious send-up of American presidential politics. Although many of the topical numbers are dated, songs like "Who Cares?" remain evergreen:

Who cares
If the sky cares to fall in the sea?
Who cares what banks fail in Yonkers,
Long as you've got a kiss that conquers,
Why should I care?
Life is one long jubilee,
So long as I care for you
And you care for me.

The penultimate line is often misquoted. Performers tend to sing "As long as I care for you." The Jeweler, ever grammatical, knew better.

In the next two years the Gershwins came up with three new shows—in the 1930s, forty musicals might open in a season—but George was restless, convinced he could take his work to a higher plane. Back in 1926 he had read *Porgy*, a poignant novel by DuBose Heyward depicting the lives of impoverished Southern blacks.

Since the debut of *Blue Monday*, the composer had itched to write a full-length "folk opera" using jazz, blues, and classical themes. Set against a backdrop of African-Americana, *Porgy* seemed to offer an ideal mix of tragedy, comedy, and ethnicity.

George anxiously arranged to meet Heyward. The novelist was not what he expected. For starters, he was a Southern white aristocrat—an ancestor had signed the Declaration of Independence. Yet Heyward had known poverty intimately, after the early death of his parents, when the traumatized boy dropped out of school and went to work on the Charleston docks. There he learned about the lives and loves of black folk and determined to write about them. *Porgy* became a best-seller and put him on the map. Heyward knew of Gershwin's work, but he too was surprised by his soon-to-be collaborator. "My first impression remains with me and is singularly vivid," the novelist wrote. "A young man of enormous physical and emotional vitality, who possessed the faculty of seeing himself quite impersonally and realistically, and who knew exactly what he wanted and where he was going. At that time he had numerous Broadway successes to his credit, and his *Rhapsody in Blue* had placed him in the front ranks of American composers. It was extraordinary, I thought, that in view of a success that might well have dazzled any man, he could appraise his talent with such complete detachment. And so we decided then that some day when we were both prepared we would do an operatic version of my simple Negro beggar of the Charleston streets."

That day came in 1935 when DuBose, Ira, and George went to work on *Porgy and Bess*. Ira's characteristically modest notes on "I Got Plenty o' Nuttin'" are instructive. DuBose took George's melody back to Charleston after discussing the subject of the song and what the words had to convey. "Two weeks later," wrote Ira, "DuBose sent me a version that had many useable lines; many, however, looked good on paper but were awkward when sung. This is no reflection on DuBose's ability. It takes years and years of experience to know that such a note cannot take such a syllable, that many a poetic line can be unsingable, that many an ordinary line fitted into the proper musical phrase can sound like a million. So on this song I did have to do a bit of 'polishing.' All in all, I'd consider this a 50-50 collaborative effort."

Since its first run at the Alvin Theater, *Porgy and Bess* has played all over the globe, with at least a dozen revivals in New York, including one at the Metropolitan Opera House. But its debut proved short-lived. Most key reviewers held the work at arm's length. Composer/critic Virgil Thomson wrote that "Gershwin does not even know what an opera is"; others called *Porgy* "a hybrid" and "an aggrandized musical show." The notices kept the public away. Although the Alvin slashed ticket prices, the cast still played to half-filled houses, and after 124 performances the final curtain rang down.

Emotionally drained, the Gershwins treated themselves to separate vacations. George went to Mexico, Ira and Lenore cruised to Trinidad. They returned, says George's most scrupulous biographer, Edward Jablonski, to find that "word had begun to trickle eastward that Hollywood was interested in the Gershwins"—again. Yet the interested parties feared that George might consider himself above the cinema. George sent an assuring wire to his agent: "Rumors about highbrow music ridiculous . . . am out to write hits."

That he was. RKO assigned the Gershwins to score *Shall We Dance*, starring their old colleague Fred Astaire and his partner on six earlier pictures, Ginger Rogers. Dance critic Arlene Croce notes: "No dancers ever reached a wider public, and the stunning fact is that Astaire and Rogers, whose love scenes were their dances, became the most popular team the movies have ever known." This team embodied the Gershwin spirit—their romantic tribulations solved in upbeat numbers; their unforced sophistication gilding everything they touched; their cool, witty, wholly American good humor whisking the clouds away. Like George and Ira, they made everything seem fluent, effortless. It was the kind of ease that could only come after months of labor and attention to detail.

No wonder that practically every number was a smash. Astaire took "They All Laughed" and ran:

They all laughed at Christopher Columbus
When he said the World was round.
They all laughed when Edison recorded sound. . . .
They all said we never could be happy,
They laughed at us—and how!
But ho, ho, ho!
Who's got the last laugh now?

In his memoir, *Lyrics on Several Occasions*, Ira recalls the song's genesis. "In the Twenties not only the stock market but the self-improvement business boomed. One dance-school advertisement, for instance, featured, 'They all laughed when I sat down to play the piano.' So the phrase 'they all laughed' germinated and estivated in the back of my mind for a dozen years until the right climate and tune popped it out as a title."

"Let's Call the Whole Thing Off," with its cascade of pronunciations, became another audience favorite:

You say eether and I say eyether,
You say neether and I say nyther;
Eether, eyether, neether, nyther—
Let's call the whole thing off.

And "They Can't Take That Away from Me" entered the pantheon of cinematic love songs:

We may never, never meet again
On the bumpy road to love,
Still I'll always, always keep
The mem'ry of—

The way you hold your knife,
The way we danced til three,
The way you changed my life—
No, no, they can't take that away from me.

As Alec Wilder shrewdly observes in his definitive *American Popular Song*, the depression years marked the Gershwins' greatest popularity. And since George was "rarely given to sad songs, what could have been a more welcome palliative for the natural gloom of the times than the consistently insistently cheery sound of his music?"

It went on cheering in George and Ira's next film, *A Damsel in Distress*, again starring Astaire. "A Foggy Day (in London Town)" quickly climbed the Hit Parade, and "Nice Work If You Can Get It," with its conflation of employment and romance, became a depression anthem:

The man who lives for only making money
Lives a life that isn't necessarily sunny;
Likewise the man who works for fame—
There's no guarantee that time won't erase his name.
The fact is
The only work that really brings enjoyment
Is the kind that is for girl and boy meant.
Fall in love—you won't regret it.
That's the best work of all—if you can get it.

Holding hands at midnight
'Neath a starry sky. . . .
Nice work if you can get it,
And you can get it—if you try.

By now George had seen and heard his "serious" work—*Concerto in F, Variations on "I Got Rhythm," Preludes for Piano, An American in Paris*—performed in the major concert halls of Europe and the United States. He had more such projects in mind, but the easy life in California quickly seduced him. He took up oil painting and tennis, and started work on yet another film. After all, he reasoned, he had plenty of time to compose longer pieces; he was only thirty-eight. For the *Goldwyn Follies*, he and Ira wrote some numbers that displeased the studio, and one song that audiences soon knew by heart:

It's very clear
Our love is here to stay
Not for a year,
But ever and a day.

The radio and the telephone
And the movies that we know
May just be passing fancies—
And in time may go.
But oh, my dear,
Our love is here to stay.
Together we're
Going a long, long way.

In time the Rockies may crumble,
Gibraltar may tumble
(They're only made of clay),
But—our love is here to stay.

Alas, there would be no more time for anything. "Love Is Here to Stay" is the last song George Gershwin ever wrote. He had experienced memory lapses during some piano recitals, and in the spring of 1937 suffered from blinding headaches. In the early summer his personality underwent a disturbing change. Behrman dropped in at the composer's Beverly Hills home. "It was not the George we all knew," he remembered. "He was very pale. The light had gone from his eyes. He seemed old.

"I asked him if he felt pain.

"'Behind my eyes,' he said, and repeated it: 'behind my eyes.' I knelt beside him on the sofa and put my hand under his head. I asked if he felt like playing the piano. He shook his head. It was the first refusal I'd ever heard from him.

"'I had to live for this,' he said, 'that Sam Goldwyn should say to me: "Why don't you write hits like Irving Berlin?"'"

Originally dismissed as psychosomatic, the symptoms indicated a grave illness, disclosed when George took an afternoon nap on July 7 and fell into a coma. Brain specialists arrived, and operated the following day. They removed a grapefruit-size tumor, but the damage was fatal: George died on the morning of July 11. "His death seems to me the most tragic thing I have ever known," wrote George S. Kaufman. As the body went back east by rail, radio stations continually played Gershwin songs. George was buried in Westchester on a rainy July 15, after simultaneous overcrowded services at Temple Emanu-El in New York and B'nai Brith Temple in Hollywood. Earlier, Mayor Fiorello LaGuardia had ordered a two-minute memorial silence, observed throughout the five boroughs. Subways stopped in their tracks, as did buses, taxis, and pedestrians. It was as if the nation wanted to freeze the clock forever. Only later could George's friends console themselves, much as A. E. Housman did with the poem "To an Athlete, Dying Young":

Smart lad, to slip betimes away
From fields where glory does not stay
And early though the laurel grows
It withers quicker than the rose.

Behrman's memoir is one of many restatements of that theme: "I see that George lived all his life in youth. He was 38 when he died. He was given no time for the middle years, for the era when you look back, when you reflect, when you regret. His rhythms were the pulsations of youth. He reanimated them in those much older than he was. He reanimates them still."

But for Ira, no words sufficed to express his state of mind. It was as if he had lost one of his hands. Because he remained under contract to Sam Goldwyn and because he believed in professionalism over self-indulgence, he completed the rest of the songs for the *Follies*. Vernon Duke composed the new tunes. En route, says Ira's biographer Philip Furia, Duke "took down a melody Ira sang for a verse for 'Love Is Here to Stay'"; Ira's lyric registers his own distraught state of mind:

The more I read the papers,
The less I comprehend
The world and all its capers
And how it all will end.
Nothing seems to be lasting. . . .

The next months were a blur of melancholy. Then one day, Ira recalled, "I got to the record player and somehow found myself putting on the Fred Astaire recordings of the *Shall We Dance* score—most of which had been written in that very room less than a year before. In a few moments the room was filled with gaiety and rhythm, and I felt that George, smiling and approving, was there listening with me—and grief vanished."

Grief would return in waves, though, and three years passed before Ira went back into harness. This time it was with composer Kurt Weill, a refugee from Nazi Germany. Weill had collaborated with Bertolt Brecht during the Weimar period, composing the music for stinging cabaret operas like *The Threepenny Opera* and *Rise and Fall of the City of Mahagonny*. In the United States, he found work on Broadway, writing *Knickerbocker Holiday* with Maxwell Anderson, a show that featured Weill's first American hit, "September Song." Playwright/director Moss Hart sought the composer out for a new kind of project. Having undergone psychoanalysis, Hart envisioned an unconventional demi-opera about the id, the ego, and the superego, full of dream sequences and subconscious revelations. Weill was his first choice to write the music, but who would supply the lyrics? Lorenz Hart? Drank too much. Oscar Hammerstein II? Too sentimental. What about Ira Gershwin? He fired off a telegram, explaining his idea. Ira thought about it for days, realized that he had stagnated for too long, and signed on to write the rhymes for the musical, then entitled *I Am Listening*.

By the time Hart's show opened at the Colonial in 1941, it had a new title: *Lady in the Dark*. The musical focused on the tribulations of a neurotic women's magazine editor, played by Gertrude Lawrence, and the dreams that revealed her inner conflicts. The tender ballad "My Ship" enjoyed immediate popularity; a punning song about marriage, "It's Never Too Late to Mendelssohn," announced that Ira's wit was intact, and the patter song "Tchaikowsky" made a star of an unknown, Danny Kaye, when he rattled off the names of more than fifty Russian composers in less than a minute. The final stanza always drew an ovation that lasted longer than the number itself:

There's Liadoff and Karganoff,
Markievitch, Pantschenko

And Dargomyzski, Stcherbatcheff,
Scriabine, Vassilenko,
Stravinsky, Rimsky-Korsakoff,
Mussorgsky, and Gretchaninoff
And Glazounoff and Caesar Cui,
Kalinikoff, Rachmaninoff,

Stravinsky and Gretchaninoff
Rumshinsky and Rachmaninoff,
I really have to stop, the subject has been dwelt
Upon enough!

Lady in the Dark ran for two years and in 1944 became a major film vehicle for Ginger Rogers. But Ira didn't capitalize on his most recent success. For the next several years, he noted, "I did little else but read, answer letters and turn down scripts." Moving from flat to flat in his youth, coupled with the back-and-forth of Beverly Hills to Broadway as an adult, had left its mark. Even though Ira considered himself "a New Yorker first and last," he and Lenore settled into a big house in Beverly Hills, where they would spend the rest of their lives. Hollywood seemed right for him; in 1945 MGM produced *Rhapsody in Blue*, a worshipful, inaccurate screen biography of George Gershwin. Robert Alda (Alan's father) played the composer rather listlessly, but no matter: the music was glorious, and the public ate it up. Once again, George's soaring melodies and irresistible beats filled the airwaves.

From here on, Ira would work with the "A" list of American popular composers—Harold Arlen, Jerome Kern, Burton Lane, Arthur Schwartz, Harry Warren—yet he would write for Broadway only twice more, and neither occasion turned out well. The first show, *The Firebrand of Florence*, began happily; he and Kurt Weill based it on Benvenuto Cellini's delightfully indiscreet memoirs. Many of the songs saluted Ira's idol, W. S. Gilbert:

We're soldiers of a duchy
Whose Duke is very touchy,
Exploding on the slightest provocation.
The ducal front we back up,
And we're supposed to hack up
The enemies who cause him aggravation.
Night and day we have to drill—
He doesn't like us standing still.

But the public, weary of war, had already turned away from the past, toward modern sounds and contemporary thoughts. *Firebrand* closed after forty-three performances. Bowing to the zeitgeist, Ira next worked with Arthur Schwartz on a "so-called 'smart' show" about divorce, with a gag-filled book by George S. Kaufman. During the Boston tryout of *Park Avenue*, a friend of Schwartz's saw the show gratis. "She cried through most of it," Ira recalled. "She had recently been divorced and just couldn't take it." Neither could the New York audience. "No-fault" divorces had yet to enter the lexicon of meaningless jargon. In those less irresponsible days, a marital split was no laughing matter, and no singing one either. The musical closed after seventy-two performances. "Heigh-ho," the lyricist wrote a friend, "guess I can't afford to do any more flops—two in a row is about six too many."

Ira returned to film work, composing rhymes to his brother's unpublished "trunk" music for the Ginger Rogers vehicle *The Shocking Miss Pilgrim*. This too flopped. Ira announced his retirement. At fifty, he said, he was "determined to rest."

He would break that rest several times. He collaborated with Harry Warren on *The Barkleys of Broadway*, the last film to star Astaire and Rogers. It was not easy. P. G. Wodehouse once told Ira that the greatest challenge in lyric writing was to come across a section of melody requiring three double rhymes. In "Shoes with Wings On," that was exactly what Ira encountered. "I well realized what this special torture was," he wrote, "when I tackled 'wings on.' When I finally wound up with 'wings on—strings on—things on,' I felt like a suddenly unburdened Atlas":

I give Aladdin the lamp,
Midas the gold.
Who needs a wizard or magician
In the old tradition?
That's not competition—
I've got 'em beat by a thousandfold!
Why?

'Cause I've got shoes with wings on—
And living has no strings on.
I put those magic things on,
And I go flying with 'em
And the town is full of rhythm
And the world's in rhyme.

But these were minor triumphs in a career rapidly winding down. Gene Kelly's 1951 film, *An American in Paris*, with its sweet Gershwin tunes, reminded the world of how much it had lost in 1939. The melodies, at once heartbreakingly beautiful and jaunty, evoked a long-gone romantic era, a time before irony and doubt had replaced wit and feeling. It reminded Ira, too, of how lonely he had been all these years. In palmier days he had written a British-tinged song:

Stiff upper lip! Stout fella!
When you're in a stew—
Sober or blotto,

This is your motto:
Keep muddling through!

Now he took the words seriously, muddling through as best he could, aware that the Jeweler was not much in demand.

And then, in 1954, Warner Bros. assigned him to work with Harold Arlen on the Judy Garland film *A Star Is Born*. "The Man That Got Away" came from this coupling, and with the exception of "Over the Rainbow," with Arlen's music and Yip Harburg's lyrics, no other song has ever been so identified with the singer; it became an integral part of every Garland concert. Her phrases gave desperation a human face:

The night is bitter,
The stars have lost their glitter;
The winds grow colder
And suddenly you're older—
And all because of the man that got away.

No more his eager call,
The writing's on the wall;
The dreams you've dreamed have all
Gone astray.

Typically, Ira had a reason for the ungrammatical title—"that" instead of "who." This "had to be 'The Man That Got Away,'" he explained, "because, actually, the title hit me as a paraphrase of the angler's 'You should have seen the one that got away.'"

After *A Star Is Born* came some undistinguished efforts—*The Country Girl* in 1954; *Kiss Me, Stupid* ten years later. Between these films Ira tended to the things that mattered most to him: editing and annotating the works of George and Ira Gershwin. In the course of his activities he came across an unused song, "I'm a

Poached Egg," for *Shall We Dance*. He set new words to it, in the style of a Cole Porter "list" song:

I'm a poached egg
Without a piece of toast,
Yorkshire pudding without a beef to roast,
A haunted house
That hasn't got a ghost—
When I'm without you.

I'm a lawyer
Who never won a case,
I'm a missile
That can't get into space,
Just a poached egg
With egg upon its face—
Each time I'm without you.

In one sense, it was just a job, a comic tune for Dean Martin to warble in a second-rate farce. In another, it was an expression of Ira's state of mind, kept from sight and sound since his brother's death.

Ira went on puttering with items in the Gershwin estate, always modest to a fault. Whenever a tribute occurred, he always seemed astonished. After a Beltway celebration of the brothers, he asked a friend, "Did you ever think you'd see the day that Ira Gershwin would be a guest of the Library of Congress?"

He died peacefully in 1983 at eighty-five, still organizing memoirs of the past. Just how he felt about rock 'n' roll and rap, heavy metal, and the rest of the pop parade went unrecorded. But one can imagine. These are the days when the three double rhymes of Chamillionaire's chant have become: "Next to the PlayStation controller / There's a full clip in my pistola / Turn a jacker into a coma." And when Bon Jovi gets standing ovations for singing, "When the world keeps trying to drag me down, / I've gotta raise my hands, gonna stand my ground. / Well I say, Have a nice day." A jeweler would be out of place in this environment, on the Broadway that houses *Spamalot* and in the Hollywood that produced *The Producers*.

We are all poached eggs now.

The Voodoo That He Did So Well

When Groucho Marx wondered if a joke was too sophisticated, he would ask his brothers, "What'll this mean to the barber in Peru?" The comedian wasn't referring to the South American nation; he meant Peru, Indiana—his notion of Hick Town, U.S.A. But *that* Peru turned out to be a most inappropriate choice. Unbeknownst to Groucho, it was the birthplace of New York City's most urbane resident: Cole Albert Porter.

Born in 1891, Cole Porter was the only surviving child of pharmacist Samuel Porter and Catherine "Kate" Cole. The family never worried about making ends meet. Cole's maternal grandfather, real estate speculator and businessman James Omar Cole, was the wealthiest man in Indiana, and his imperious manner showed it. Little Cole, cosseted from birth, flourished in a home dominated by his humorless grandfather and his ambitious mother. His father seems mostly a cipher in his life.

Kate made sure her son had every advantage available to a small-town child, including music lessons. The instruction wasn't wasted: by six the little southpaw could play complicated piano and violin solos; by ten he wrote the music and lyrics of his first number, "Song of the Birds." Mama, convinced she had produced a *wunderkind*, arranged for Cole to play piano and violin concerts in and around Peru. She lopped a year off his age to make him seem even more prodigious to credulous Hoosiers.

Her aspirations exacted a high price. Cole became withdrawn and unpopular. "Other children didn't mix much with Cole," recalled a neighbor. "His mother dressed him up like Lord Fauntleroy and other children made fun of him. Cole was very shy as a boy." Ironically, by the time the boy had overcome his shyness and learned to entertain an audience, it became clear that he didn't possess the right stuff for Carnegie Hall. As the ovations ebbed—there were other, more gifted young musicians in Indiana—doting Kate at last conceded that her son would have to pursue another line of work.

In the early twentieth century the wealthy sent their sons east to be educated, and soon after his fourteenth birthday in 1905, the slender, undersize Porter enrolled in elite Worcester Academy in Massachusetts. The school's dean, a Dr. Abercrombie, was famous for his aphorisms: "Democracy is not a leveling down, but a leveling up," for example, and "A gentleman never eats. He breakfasts, he lunches, he dines, but he never eats." Abercrombie, familiar with grand opera and the popular songs of the day, taught Porter an important music lesson. "Words and music," he advised, "must be so inseparably wedded to each other that they are like one."

The formerly shy boy also began to exhibit a powerful charm. In his senior year, Porter chastely courted Beulah Mae Singer, who remembered him years later as attractive, even though he "wasn't what you could call handsome." In fact "he moved like a frisky monkey and looked like a solemn bullfrog with slightly buggy eyes," she recalled. But Porter captured her heart "by sheer force of personality."

That force remained with him when he entered Yale in 1910. At first, some of his classmates found him off-putting. Gerald Murphy, later a friend of F. Scott Fitzgerald's and the subject of the best-selling *Living Well Is the Best Revenge*, remembered meeting the new Eli. "Sitting at the piano was a little boy from Peru, Indiana, in a checkered suit and a salmon tie, looking just like a Westerner dressed up for the East." Porter "did not fit easily into the social mold of a Yale man," Murphy dryly added. But Murphy soon found himself won over by the pianist, as was almost everyone who met him. Porter's seemingly limitless verve was the source of his charm. "I am the most enthusiastic person in the world," he liked to say. "I like everything as long as it's different." By different, he meant new, offbeat, fresh—and a sexual preference that diverged from the classic image of the Yale man.

Cole's Yale years were musical. He sang in the Whiffenpoofs, led the glee club, created class musicals, and came up with rallying cries for the football team. Two of his cheerleading exhortations—"Bingo Eli Yale" and "Bulldog" (Bulldog! Bow wow wow!)—are sung to this day. He also penned in 1913 the first of his "list" songs. "As I Love You" presented a lover's past conquests and present darling:

Esmerelda,
Then Griselda,
And the third was Rosalie.
Lovely Lakme
Tried to track me,
But I fell for fair Marie.
Eleanora

Followed Dora,
Then came Eve with eyes of blue.
But I swear I ne'er loved any girl
As I love you.

In his senior year, Porter toured America with the glee club, and his original songs—almost all of them funny—won rave reviews. A Cincinnati paper wrote: "Cole Porter appeared in the program but once, but when the audience had him there they wouldn't let him go until his stock of 10 or 12 encores was exhausted." Serious music and rah-rah songs were all very well, but it was humor that won the big applause, Porter now realized. Comedy, almost unknown in his stern childhood home in Peru, was the most desirable asset an entertainer could possess. Be a clown, he later observed: "All the world loves a clown. / Show 'em tricks, tell 'em jokes / And you'll only stop with top folks."

Yet if Cole Porter became a joke teller, he was a sophisticated one. Throughout his Yale years he kept scribbling in notebooks, now in his alma mater's custody. One entry examined Lord Byron, whose libertine life and poetic license Porter clearly admired. "He was free to change his mood," wrote Porter, "from flippancy to poetry, from beauty to obscenity." Porter's music would soon cover a comparably expansive range of human emotions, always with Byron's urbanity and often with his flamboyant, daredevil rhymes.

The wildly successful Yale Glee Club tour introduced Porter's dual performing persona: a vaudevillian who could bring down the house, and an elegant who could amuse because he wanted to, not because he had to. Ever afterward he described himself as a "cross between Eddie Cantor and the Duke of Windsor."

After graduation Porter, at his father's urging, entered Harvard Law School. A fellow student recalled the epochal day the professor called on Porter to discuss a landmark case. Porter obviously hadn't prepared. The prof "leaned over his desk and very superciliously said, 'Mr. Porter, why don't you learn to play the fiddle?' and Cole Porter got up, walked out of the class and never went back to Harvard Law School." He didn't walk far, however: he transferred to Harvard's School of Music. Looking back, Porter observed that if older and wiser men "hadn't been so sure I would never become a judge in law—I might never have become such a good judge in other things."

By 1915, Porter's mother, acknowledging that he would never have his name engraved on a legal firm's letterhead, urged him to try his hand at songwriting. Promptly exchanging New England for New York, he managed to sell a few numbers for a Junior League show. He enthusiastically wrote home: "Tell granddad [that producer] Lew Fields gave me $50 for each song I sold him, and four cents on each copy."

The following year Porter found a backer for his Broadway debut, *See America First*. What would be a long love affair between Cole Porter and New York City got off to a rocky start: *See America First*—a derivative, Gilbert and Sullivan–style musical comedy, according to Robert Kimball, who has reconstructed the work from fragments and scattered reports—flopped ignominiously. Savaged by critics, the show closed after fifteen performances, mortifying Porter. "As they dismantled the scenery and trucked it out of the stage alley," he later recalled, "I honestly believed I was disgraced for the rest of my life."

By then the guns of August had fired, and World War I provided Porter with an excuse to leave town. He encouraged the legend that he had joined the French Foreign Legion during the war. In truth he worked for an American relief organization, visited towns ravaged by the Germans, and eventually joined the American Expeditionary Forces, quartered in Paris (though he saw no battle).

After the armistice, Porter stayed on in the City of Light, taking an occasional class in composition, writing an occasional ballad, amusing acquaintances and friends with occasional performances, and moving with the *haute monde*. Novelist Michael Arlen, another expatriate, wrote a caricature of Porter in 1919. "Every morning at half-past seven Cole Porter leaps lightly out of bed and having said his prayers, arranges himself in a riding habit. Then, having written a song or two, he will appear at the stroke of half-past twelve at the Ritz, where leaning in a manly way on the bar, he will say 'Champagne cocktail, please. Had a marvelous ride this morning.' That statement gives him strength and confidence on which to suffer this, our life, until ten minutes past three in the afternoon when he will fall into a childlike sleep."

Porter was adrift. But the same year Arlen poked fun at him, Porter met someone who would change his life forever and help him find direction: Linda Lee Thomas, an affluent divorcée several years his senior. Within three months they announced their engagement. Distant relatives and acquaintances beamed on this union of wealth and wit. Insiders scratched their heads: they knew that Porter was homosexual. He had kept his liaisons secret at Yale, but several undergrads knew the nature of his friendship with Monty Woolley, a drama instructor and later a celebrated character actor. During Porter's senior year the two men would cruise together, picking up sailors. According to one story, a seaman spotted them in their car and inquired, "Are you guys fags?" Replied Woolley, "Now that the preliminaries are over, why don't you get in and we can discuss the financial details."

Nevertheless the marriage took. Linda's first husband, Edward Thomas, had abused her. ("An automobile enthusiast," notes biographer William McBrien, Thomas "had the distinction of being the first American to kill someone in an automobile accident.") Linda wanted no part of marriage as she had known it. As long as her second husband kept his trysts private and emotionally uninvolving, she was willing to look the other way. For his part, Porter tried never to embarrass his chic, blue-blooded wife—though he stepped over the line more than once. Of greater importance to Linda and to Cole was his songwriter vocation. Would he recover from his Broadway failure, or would he go on squandering his life in Europe's spas and *boîtes*, just another bon vivant?

He certainly would have the means to squander his life away. On a visit to Manhattan in 1923, Porter learned that his wealthy grandfather had just died, at ninety-four. "I was not mentioned in Grandfather's will," Porter later noted. "But he left my mother over two million dollars and she generously gave me half of it—with the remark that she wanted me to feel completely independent." A few years later the will gave Porter's mother $2 million more, and she again gave her only son half.

Clearly Porter agreed with Somerset Maugham's aperçu: "Money is like a sixth sense, without which one cannot make use of the other five." He proceeded to live a luxurious, but not totally indulgent, life. While he partied in Europe, he continued to learn his craft, and he entertained musicians others would not. Impresario Boris Kochno-Diaghilev grumbled to a friend: "The whole of Venice is up in arms against Cole Porter because of his jazz and his Negroes. They are teaching the Charleston on the Lido Beach! It's dreadful!"

With his wife's encouragement, Porter gradually edged back into show business, writing songs that announced the arrival of a new and formidable talent. Indeed, one song caught the spirit of Noel Coward's bittersweet plays so well that Noel flattered Cole by writing a parody, gently poking fun at their shared homosexuality. The Porter version:

Weren't we fools to lose each other?
Weren't we fools to say goodbye?
Tho' we know we loved each other,
You chose another,
So did I.

The Coward send-up:

Weren't we fools to lose each other?
Though we know we loved each other
You chose your brother,
So did I.

New York audiences got an inkling of the Cole to come in *Paris*, a lighthearted revue that opened in 1928 at Irving Berlin's Music Box Theater and featured a throwaway number called "Let's Do It." With this list song, Porter made double entendre an art all his own:

Romantic sponges, they say, do it
Oysters, down in Oyster Bay, do it.
Let's do it, let's fall in love.
Cold Cape Cod clams, 'gainst their wish, do it,
Even lazy jellyfish do it,
Let's do it, let's fall in love.
Electric eels, I might add, do it,
Though it shocks 'em, I know,
Why ask if shad do it?

Waiter, bring me shad roe.
In shallow shoals, English soles do it,
Goldfish in the privacy of bowls, do it,
Let's do it, let's fall in love.

But it was with the 1929 opening of *Fifty Million Frenchmen* at the Lyric Theater that Porter really arrived. Not all the reviews were positive—the Crash had just occurred, and many found insouciance unseemly. Even so, two endorsements generated long lines at the box office: "The words and music leap lightfooted from Cole Porter"—*New York Times*; "The best musical comedy I have seen in years"—Irving Berlin.

The musical's freewheeling plot about an American in Paris proved as insubstantial as a soap bubble. One song, however, became a classic. Years before, the impresario Billy Rose had studied the lyrics of popular songs and found that the "oo" sound—as in June, moon, and spoon—showed up in more than half the hits. Inspired, he concocted the novelty number "Barney Google, with the *goo-goo—goog*ly Eyes" and saw it rise to the top of the charts in 1923. The lesson wasn't lost on Porter. But his song "You Do Something to Me" demonstrates the difference between the shrewd craftsman and the authentic poet. For Porter did more than repeat an agreeable sound; he made it an incantation in E flat:

Let me live 'neath your spell
Do do that voodoo that you do so well,
For you do something to me
That nobody else could do.

Porter wrapped the words in a seductive tune that never wearies listeners. Such elusive, unforgettable melodies would be a hallmark of his style.

After *Fifty Million Frenchmen* came a flood of shows and songs that definitively established Porter's reputation as a musical genius. The time was right for his brand of urbane intelligence. This was an era of smartening up, not dumbing down. In Manhattan, *The New Yorker* and *Time* were invigorating journalism with what H. L. Mencken called the American Language. As if to defy the depression, newspapers put a premium on cleverness, challenging readers with ballades and triolets, rhyming versions of operas, travelogues in verse. Cosmopolitans thirsted for culture; they wanted to know more tomorrow than they did yesterday. It was a time when the skyline of New York was the national expression of optimism—when the breadlines lengthened but musicals were elegant; when booze was forbidden, hence twice as intoxicating; when the Chrysler Building and Rockefeller Center were going up and everyone felt the way Jay Gatsby and Nick Carraway did when they drove from Manhattan and Nick observed: "The city seen from the Queensboro Bridge is always the city seen for the first time, in its first wild promise of all the mystery and the beauty in the world."

To produce great popular art, you need a gifted artist, a receptive audience, and a high state of civilization. Cole Porter's New York had all three. In his words and music, Porter distilled the city's striving spirit and its collective intelligence. As John Updike explains: "Wit of a particularly literary sort lay behind Cole Porter's sophisticated references and outrageous rhymes—'trickery / liquor we,' 'throws a / sub rosa,' 'presto / West, oh,' 'Siena / then a.'" His listeners hung on to every syllable.

But there was something else they hung on to too, something darker and more provocative. In *The New Yorkers*, Porter dared to write a hit song about a prostitute in the clinical manner of a naturalistic novel. One can visualize the world-weary demimondaine, several steps ahead of her client, her seamed stockings illuminated by a bare lightbulb:

When the only sound in the empty street
Is the heavy tread of the heavy feet
That belong to a lonesome cop,
I open shop. . . .
Let the poets pipe of love
In their childish way,
I know ev'ry type of love
Better far than they.
If you want the thrill of love,
I've been through the mill of love,
Old love, new love,
Ev'ry love but true love. . . .
If you want to buy my wares
Follow me and climb the stairs,
Love for sale.

Porter balanced the dark "Love for Sale" with a song that indulgently celebrated the city of skyscrapers and speakeasies, quarts and all.

I like the city air, I like to drink of it,
The more I know New York, the more I think of it
I like the sight and the sound and even the stink of it.

Theater people now realized that the amusing little chap at the keyboard was no dilettante; Cole Porter was changing the course of American popular song. Take, as another example, "Night and Day," introduced in 1932 by the young Fred Astaire in *The Gay Divorcee*—gay, in those benighted days, meaning blithe. The melody, as fellow songwriter Alec Wilder remarked, "is so beautifully fashioned it may, indeed, have been preceded by a blueprint." The words expressed a carnality rarely found in "serious" odes of the period, let alone in popular song. Ring Lardner, a close student of popular culture, wrote that "with 'Night and Day' Mr. Porter makes a monkey of his contemporaries, and he does it with one couplet"—

Night and day under the hide of me
There's an, Oh, such a hungry yearning burning inside of me.

Admiration didn't stop Lardner from crafting several parodies, including "Night and day under the bark of me / There's an, Oh, such a mob of microbes making a park of me" and "Night and day under my tegument / There's a voice telling me, I'm he, the good little egg you meant." Porter himself must have been pleased with the song: he wore a pair of cuff links with the moon enameled on one side, the sun on the other—night and day.

Following *The Gay Divorcee*, Porter outdid himself—and every other Broadway composer—in the 1933 Broadway smash *Anything Goes*. The title song alone would have reinforced his reputation as the sexiest composer alive:

Good authors too who once knew better words
Now only use four-letter words
Writing prose,
Anything goes.
If driving fast cars you like,
If low bars you like,
If old hymns you like,
If bare limbs you like,
If Mae West you like,
Or me undressed you like,

Why, nobody will oppose.
When ev'ry night, the set that's smart is in-
Truding in nudist parties in
Studios,
Anything goes.

Porter explored other uncharted territory in his lyrics. Ticket holders at the Alvin Theater had barely settled into their seats when the previously verboten subject of drug use came up in a song:

Some get a kick from cocaine.
I'm sure that if I took even one sniff
That would bore me terrific'ly too
Yet I get a kick out of you.

Porter's innovations were formal too. Audacious internal rhymes became a signature: "Flying on *high* with some *guy* in the *sky* is my *i*-dea of nothing to do." His use of triplets dazzled audiences then as they do today: "I used to fall / In love with all / Those boys who maul / Refined ladies / But now I tell / Each young gazelle / To go to hell / I mean Hades." So does his use of cadence: "Like the drip, drip, drip of the raindrops when the summer shower is through / So a voice within me keeps repeating, You—You—You," and caesura, lines dictated by the natural rhythm of the language: "Most gentlemen don't like love, they just like to kick it around / Most gentlemen don't like love, 'cause most gentlemen can't be profound." Perhaps the ultimate salute came not from audiences but anthologists: *The Oxford Book of American Light Verse* placed his works, sans music, alongside that of such masters as T. S. Eliot, e. e. cummings, and Ogden Nash.

The nadir of the depression, 1933, was a peak year in Porter's career; it was also when he and Linda, after years of exile in

Europe, set down deep roots in New York City, moving lock, stock, dachshund, cat, and two grand pianos into the forty-first floor of the Waldorf Towers, their Gotham address for the rest of their lives. (When the dog and cat eventually died, the Porters replaced them with a pair of new felines: one named Anything, the other Goes.) Ensconced at the Waldorf, Porter worked every day for hours; then he would present himself to the public as a bon vivant, regularly attending Manhattan society soirees and high-toned entertainments. The image he conveyed was of a man who could effortlessly dash off all 108 measures of "Begin the Beguine" between cocktail parties.

The cultivated image of the songwriter as epicure proved so convincing that it outlasted even the *annus horribilis* of 1937. Cole and Linda weren't getting along by now; she was in France, mulling over divorce. Cole was horseback riding with friends at an Oyster Bay estate when his high-strung mount, frightened by something in the woods, reared abruptly and fell over on its rider. The accident so severely damaged Porter's legs that doctors wanted to amputate them. Word of the catastrophe reached Linda; she sent a wire forbidding the drastic operation and hastened to her husband's bedside. Only her intervention kept the physicians from carrying out their plans. From then on, there was no more talk of divorce.

Years before, Porter had written "Don't Fence Me In," about a cowpoke for whom freedom was oxygen:

I want to ride to the ridge where the West commences,
Gaze at the moon till I lose my senses,
Can't look at hobbles and I can't stand fences,
Don't fence me in.

Hobbles: *Noun. Devices used to slow down or restrain an animal.* The dreaded restraints—crutches and canes—were what Porter would face from now on, and he knew it.

In excruciating pain, Porter could easily have forsaken songwriting at this point: he had money in overplus, Linda's renewed dedication, an aerie in the town he adored. Yet that wasn't Cole Porter's way. He was a gentleman; gentlemen do not give in to affliction. A friend reported that during his convalescence Porter took some "14 different kinds of narcotics and hypnotics and sedatives daily. And there was great fear that when he did get out of the hospital he'd have to go on a cure." Instead he kicked his habits, including an almost hourly belladonna pill, and got back to work.

Porter refused to become an invalid, working his way around the apartment by hanging on to the furniture, employing two canes when he had to walk outside, or, in difficult moments, getting one of his brawny menservants to carry him from room to room. Dramatist Bella Spewak, working with Porter on a show called *Leave It to Me* during this convalescence, offers a vivid image of the songsmith. He was, she wrote, "small, dapper, with black velvet eyes and a ready, winsome smile." The crippled composer "rose with the aid of crutches to meet us," she recalled. "I don't want to give the impression that he just tossed off songs like 'My Heart Belongs to Daddy,' for we knew better, but he certainly gave us that impression. And the tossing off, he would have you believe, came between and during bouts of pain."

By 1939 Porter felt well enough to visit Hollywood for a while. To him, spending time in the movie colony was "like living on the moon," but he needed a lunar break. Among a half-dozen songs he penned for the Fred Astaire movie *Broadway Melody of 1940*, Porter sent a fresh love letter to his favorite New York thoroughfare:

Glorify Sixth Avenue
And put bathrooms in the zoo,
But please don't monkey with Broadway.
Put big floodlights in the park,

And put Harlem in the dark,
But please don't monkey with Broadway.
Though it's tawdry and plain,
It's a lovely old lane,
Full of landmarks galore and memories gay,
So move Grant's Tomb to Union Square
And put Brooklyn anywhere,
But please, please,
I beg on my knees,
Don't monkey with old Broadway.

Returned to Manhattan, Porter submitted to more agonizing operations on his mangled legs—there would be some thirty-five in all—and continued writing for old Broadway. His range remained wide. He could turn out sophisticated patter to equal anything of Noel Coward's. Here he imagines a New Yorker sardonically addressing his weekend hostess:

Thank you a lot,
And don't be surprised if you suddenly should be quietly shot
For the clinging perfume
And that damp little room,
For those cocktails so hot
And the bath that was not,
For those guests so amusing and mentally bracing
Who talked about racing and racing and racing,
For the ptomaine I got from your famous tin salmon,
For the fortune I lost when you taught me backgammon,
For those mornings I spent with your dear but deaf mother,
For those evenings I passed with that bounder, your brother,

And for making me swear to myself there and then
Never to go for a weekend again.

And he could be as simple and affecting as Irving Berlin:

You'd be so nice to come home to,
You'd be so nice by the fire,
While the breeze on high
Sang a lullaby
You'd be all that I
Could desire.

The trouble, though, was that Cole Porter had become incapable of turning out a trademark Cole Porter song, with its inimitable mix of eroticism and esprit. Perhaps it was the continual surgeries, friends theorized, or World War II, with its shift of public taste to big-band jazz and novelty numbers; or perhaps he had simply lost his focus along with his looks. For, having appeared so youthful for so long, Porter now seemed older than his years, more gnome than sprite.

Although he showed flashes of the old dazzle, fashionable opinion increasingly considered him obsolete, a back number from a bygone era. That's exactly how Warner Bros. depicted him in its fatuous 1946 biopic *Night and Day*. Cary Grant played Cole in jaunty, straight-as-a-string mode, producing hit songs with the facility of a man jingling change in his pockets. The film even showed Porter in the uniform of the French Foreign Legion, as gritty and gung ho as a *poilu*. Critics derided it mercilessly.

Porter could hardly take the blame for *Night and Day*—it was *about* him, after all, not by him. But you couldn't say the same of *Around the World in 80 Days*. In 1946, Orson Welles got it into his head that the Jules Verne novel would make a musical extravaganza. He approached Porter, who responded with surprising enthusiasm. He called Welles's project "the kind of thing one dreams about but never quite dares to attempt. I want to do something 'different.'" Different it was. But not one Porter song made the hit parade; today all are forgotten. The show closed after just seventy-five performances.

A lesser talent would have called it quits, but Cole Porter wasn't finished yet. Late in 1947 two Broadway producers approached playwright Bella Spewak, looking for an experienced writer to modernize the Bard's raucous comedy *The Taming of the Shrew*. Fondly remembering her earlier collaboration with Porter on *Leave It to Me*, she raised his name. The producers winced; the man may have been hot stuff in his time, but now he was "washed up." She kept insisting that no one else had the gift for adapting the Bard to the modern idiom. Eventually the producers gave in.

The rest is Broadway history. In *Kiss Me Kate*, Porter's range really did seem Shakespearean. He wrote a ballad entirely in the subjunctive ("Were Thine That Special Face"), used Elizabethan inversions ("Where Is the Life That Late I Led?"), and fashioned refrains that became instant classics ("Why Can't You Behave?"; "So in Love"). Moreover, the specialty numbers weren't just hilarious; they were profoundly literate. When poet W. H. Auden proclaimed *Kiss Me Kate* a greater work than *Shrew*, he had in mind songs like "Brush Up Your Shakespeare":

With the wife of the British embessida
Try a crack out of "Troilus and Cressida."
If she says she won't buy it or tike it
Make her tike it, what's more, "As You Like It."
If she says your behavior is heinous
Kick her right in the "Coriolanus."

A *Hollywood Reporter* critic spoke for all his colleagues: "King Cole has made a monkey out of the mourners. The champ is back again." Audiences agreed: *Kate* ran for more than a thousand performances on the Main Stem and toured for the next decade. Saluted with a two-hour television special, Porter reflected, "To a person who has talent, and is willing to work hard, Broadway is as friendly as Main Street in Peru, Indiana." Although Porter's subsequent shows—*Out of This World, Can-Can,* and *Silk Stockings*—never quite equaled his greatest achievement, he kept at it, turning out melodies and rhymes that no one else could compose.

Perhaps Porter might have scaled the highest heights again, but in the mid-1950s a series of catastrophes struck him. First came the death of Kate Cole in 1952; two years later he lost Linda. "I've had two great women in my life," he said shortly after Linda's death. "My mother, who thought I had this talent, and my wife, who kept goading me along, in spite of the feeling that I couldn't appeal to the general public." In the end, the Porters' arrangement was oddly but deeply affectionate: beyond all his walking instruments and aids, Linda had become his most reliable crutch.

In 1958 amputation was no longer avoidable. After visiting Porter, Noel Coward wrote a friend, "It is a cruel decision to have to make and involves much sex vanity and many fears of being repellent. However, it is done at last and I am convinced that his whole life will cheer up and that his work will profit accordingly."

Coward couldn't have been more wrong. Porter lost the humor that had sustained him through the tribulations, began drinking hard, slid into melancholia, and never worked again. Every now and then he would dine with friends, but the conversation lacked spark and substance. "It was sad seeing him so depressed," singer Ethel Merman said, "knowing in your heart that he no longer wanted to live."

He did live on until 1964, when the combined effects of alcohol and pneumonia killed him. He died in Santa Monica, on another sojourn to the Coast. His body, flown back to Mount Hope Cemetery in Peru, Indiana, took its final resting place beside Linda's. The large and laudatory obituaries all observed that a giant had passed.

The greatest tribute, however, continues to come from Cole Porter's hit-hungry audience. Over four decades after his death, he remains one of the top three composers of American popular song (along with Irving Berlin and Richard Rodgers). There is no statue of Cole Porter in his beloved New York, and no city site commemorates his achievement. Yet continual monuments keep his name before us—in 2000 a widely praised revival of *Kiss Me Kate* had a successful run on Broadway, and more than a hundred recordings of Porter songs are still in print, including Ella Fitzgerald's, Blossom Dearie's, and Jerry Southern's definitive collections, and a best-selling tribute album, *Red, Hot, & Blue*, featuring U2, Iggy Pop, and other rock stars.

Should you doubt whether spirits haunt Manhattan, drop in to the Waldorf's Peacock Alley sometime and listen to one of the performers playing Porter's grand piano—a gift he bequeathed to the hotel. On a good night you can imagine its original owner accompanying a chorus of fans as they sing their salute to the Master, from *Anything Goes*:

You're the top!
You're a Waldorf salad.
You're the top!
You're a Berlin ballad.
You're the baby grand of a lady and a gent,
You're an old Dutch master,

You're Mrs. Astor,
You're Pepsodent.
You're romance,
You're the steppes of Russia,
You're the pants on a Roxy usher.
I'm a lazy lout that's just about to stop,
But if baby, I'm the bottom
You're the top.

Richard Rodgers: Enigma Variations

Based on current performances and record sales, the world's most popular songs aren't those of Schubert or Schumann, John Lennon or the latest hip-hop artist. They come courtesy of a gentleman of formal manner and formidable talent who took Broadway by storm more than half a century ago. Since the stage is an arena that the young rarely visit these days, the songs of Richard Rodgers (1902–1979) should have become mere antiques long ago, appreciated by connoisseurs but remote from contemporary taste. And yet Rodgers's works still find millions of listeners of every age and in almost every land. Over the past decade or so, six of his musicals have received opulent Broadway revivals, and two have enjoyed television restaging.

Why do Rodgers's tunes still enchant? Of course, there's the man's gift for melodic invention: had he set the Lands' End catalog to music, the results still would have made the Hit Parade. His music also has lasted because he was lucky enough to find just the right collaborators at key points in his career. But then, as composer Hector Berlioz once noted, it isn't enough to have talent to succeed; nor is luck alone sufficient: one has to have the talent for luck. This Rodgers possessed in overplus.

The second son of headstrong physician William Rodgers (born William Abraham) and his well-to-do wife, Mamie (née Levy), Richard Charles Rodgers grew up on Manhattan's West Side in what to outsiders seemed a placid upper-middle-class home. But in later years Richard's daughters recalled a darker scene. "I didn't get good feelings about family life," said Linda Rodgers. "I heard more comments about the difficult relationships and the silences that went on at meals. . . . [G]randfather would often storm out." Agreed elder sister Mary, "I think my father grew up with a lot of fear and anxiety."

Rodgers was too complex a man to have a "Rosebud"—a single childhood incident that illuminates all that follows. But one disturbing episode does stand out. One night the eight-year-old Richard awoke in excruciating pain, his right index finger swollen almost wrist-size. The boy had contracted osteomyelitis, an infection of the bone marrow. He lay in agony until his parents returned from a night out. When they inspected him, Rodgers remembered, "Pop simply got a scalpel from his office and had Mom hold me while he made one terrifying slash in the finger to allow the pus to escape." He faced the same procedure repeatedly until cured. "Local anesthetic was seldom used in those days, so what followed were eight months of torture to a small boy by well-meaning men," he bitterly recalled. Rodgers wondered if his lifelong hypochondria resulted from the memory of his father "suddenly appearing in the middle of the night to cut me savagely with a knife."

It was during his recuperation that Rodgers's love for music blossomed. He would listen, beguiled, as his mother played popular songs and operettas on the parlor Steinway. By age nine the little boy with a grownup face was attending Saturday music matinees by himself. Returning home, he would sit at that same family keyboard, picking out by ear the tunes he had heard. Soon he was inventing astonishingly mature melodies of his own. Serious piano lessons and attendance at classical concerts and operas followed.

Yet if little Richard loved classical music, he also sensed, even in those early days, that his destiny lay a bit north of the old Metropolitan Opera House. Irving Berlin, Jerome Kern, and other audacious tunesmiths were taking American popular music in exciting new directions. Rodgers longed to join their company.

William Rodgers wasn't amused by his son's musical ambitions. After all, the good doctor's elder son Morty was already a premed at Columbia, and the assumption was that Richard would follow in his brother's slipstream. It would not do to have a Rodgers slumming in show business. Tensions mounted. A family friend recalled a telling recital at the family's Long Island summer home. Richard was joyously playing the piano when the doctor's car crunched driveway gravel. "Dick, dear," Mama whispered, "here comes your Dad, so get away from the piano." Dick retreated on that occasion, but remained glued to the keyboard when his father wasn't around.

Young Rodgers invented melodies on that keyboard, not words: to realize his ambitions, he needed a lyricist. Boy, did he find one! The sixteen-year-old had heard about a swarthy, gnomelike Columbia graduate, Lorenz "Larry" Hart, who had built a reputation as a light versifier. One of Morty's pals knew the writer and arranged a meeting.

Larry Hart was the child of well-to-do immigrants. His rotund, irrepressible father, Max, was part hustler, part promoter, forever launching companies that prospered and then faltered, whereupon he'd just start another one—always staying a jump ahead of the creditors. This was one of Max's flush periods: he had set up his family in a posh West 119th Street townhouse. But commerce held no appeal for Larry, who, at age twenty-three, still lived at home, holed up in his cluttered room, spending his days translating German poetry and his nights drinking to excess.

Like Rodgers, Hart nourished dreams of glory—accomplishments in the theater that would win him fame and wealth. That's where the similarity ended, however. Rodgers had a muscular work ethic; music flowed out of him like conversation; he was handsome and, at least at this point, upbeat, attracted by—and attractive to—women. Hart was an undisciplined, unprepossessing man, whose furtive homosexual liaisons invariably ended in sorrow. Despite these differences, the young men hit it off: "I left Hart's house," Richard observed, "having acquired in one afternoon a career, a partner, a best friend and a source of permanent irritation."

The first Rodgers and Hart sessions were magic. One of the duo's earliest songs, "Any Old Place with You," even caught the attention of comedian/producer Lew Fields, who put it in his new musical, *A Lonely Romeo*, at the Rialto Theater. Rodgers and Hart would write far better material, but this number hinted at the remarkable oeuvre to come. Richard's tune simulated a driving locomotive; Larry's lyrics played with places to be visited:

From old Virginia
Or Abyssinia,
We'll go straight to Halifax.
I've got a mania
For Pennsylvania,
Even ride in London hacks.
I'll call each dude a pest
You like in Budapest,
Oh for far Peru!

I'll go to hell for ya,
Or Philadelphia,
Any old place with you.

Today teenagers are big stars; back then the only adolescents associated with the theater were ushers. The notion that a seventeen-year-old could have a song performed on Broadway was the stuff of headlines. Rodgers was beside himself, certain he had entered the on-ramp to success. His timing, though, was off: the Rialto suffered from the citywide recession in the early 1920s, and after the team's winning debut, no significant offers came their way.

His career stalled, Rodgers unenthusiastically enrolled at Columbia, following his brother's premed path. But he never stopped writing music. Because of his brief Broadway triumph, Rodgers received invitations to pen tunes for varsity shows (several boasting lyrics by that promising law student Oscar Hammerstein II). Off campus, Rodgers continued to work with Hart. They scored a slew of amateur musicals, with arch titles like *A Danish Yankee at King Tut's Court* and *Temple Bells*.

Rodgers never regretted the years (1920 through 1924) he spent pounding out such amateur works. It was during this period, after all, that he convinced his father that two Dr. Rodgerses would be enough for one family. Worn down by his younger son's doggedness, William permitted Richard to transfer from Columbia to the Institute of Musical Art (now Juilliard). But even more crucial to Rodgers's songwriting future, his amateur efforts provided him with his real musical education. "There is a great deal more to writing for the musical theater than learning notation, the meaning of a diminished seventh, or banging away at a typewriter in some lonely room," he acknowledged. Later in life he advised Broadway hopefuls "to reject at the start the idea that 'amateur' is a dirty word. . . .

[I]n the audience may be someone's uncle who knows an agent or a producer—or who may even be an agent or producer—and the amateur may have taken the first giant step toward becoming a professional."

Rodgers was speaking from his own early experience. To avoid relying on his father's largesse, which by 1924 had grown considerable, he was about to start a job as a traveling salesman, peddling children's undergarments for fifty dollars a week, when an intriguing offer came in. Some folks at the Theater Guild had caught a few of those amateur nights and, believing the composer and his lyricist ready for prime time, asked them to come up with the score for a new Broadway revue, *The Garrick Gaieties*.

Most of the numbers for that production are long forgotten, but a modest little duet became a city's anthem. The bright, catchy notes and knowing internal rhymes heralded the arrival of a new and irresistible Broadway style. "If one song can be said to have 'made' Rodgers and Hart," wrote the melodist, "it was 'Manhattan.'"

We'll have Manhattan
The Bronx and Staten
Island too.
It's lovely strolling through
The zoo.
It's very fancy
On old Delancey
Street, you know
The subway charms us so
When balmy breezes blow
To and fro
And tell me what street
Compares with Mott Street

In July?
Sweet pushcarts gliding by.
The great big city's a wondrous toy
Just made for a girl and boy.
We'll turn Manhattan
Into an isle of joy.

The reviews sang. Critic Robert Benchley called *Gaieties* "by miles the most civilized show in town." Rodgers and Hart's songs clicked "like a colonel's heels at attention," *Variety* enthused.

The team's next major musical, 1925's *Dear Enemy*, clicked louder and garnered even more attention. "Here in My Arms" stretched to an octave and a fifth in the nineteenth bar of its chorus. Even so, theater historian Gerald Boardman pointed out, the Rodgers tune somehow remained easy to sing, announcing "a departure from the tightly knit melodies of most musical comedy songs." Hart's contributions did not go unnoticed either: the rhyme of "radiant" with "lady aunt" in "I Beg Your Pardon" sent the *New York Sun* critic into transports of delight. For the rest of the decade, the duo flourished, scoring more than a dozen Broadway shows, some short-lived, others durable.

At first the two men wrote simultaneously, but soon Hart's eccentric behavior disrupted the routine. Rodgers was Mr. Punctual. Hart turned out to be, in his partner's memorable phrase, "a fellow who says he'll be at your house with the lyric at 2:00, and shows up on Friday." By the end of the twenties the melodies almost always came first, and Hart tardily fitted the words to them. But what words! What dazzling internal rhymes and verbal gymnastics!

Beans could get no keener re-
Ception in a beanery
Bless our mountain greenery
Home

Or:

Both thine eyes are cute, too–
What they do to
Me.
Hear me holler
I choose a sweet
Lolla
Palooza
In thee.

Or:

Sometimes I think
I've found my hero
But it's a queer ro-
Mance.
All that you need is a ticket.
Come on, big boy, ten cents a dance!

The Rodgers and Hart relationship became increasingly symbiotic. Whatever Hart gave his partner in those early years, noted fellow composer Alec Wilder, prompted Rodgers's "greatest invention and pellucid freshness." And what Rodgers gave Hart, says theater critic John Lahr, was "something insistent and sincere that plays against Hart's own inveterate cynicism."

That cynicism revealed itself in song after song. Hart could turn out rhymes about requited love when the occasion demanded—"With a Song in My Heart," for instance, or "The Blue Room." But his natural métier was disappointed romance and unfulfilled yearnings:

It is easy to see all right
Ev'rything's gonna be all right—
Be just dandy for ev'rybody but me.

I'm so hot and bothered that
I don't know
My elbow from my ear.
I suffer something awful
Each time you go
And much worse when
you're near.

He was my one and all
He was my why and wherefore.

My moon and sun and all,
He is the man I care for!
And now my love song is through.
It was too good to be true.

With Rodgers and Hart ruling Broadway, Richard took on a different kind of partner. The daughter of a prominent New York lawyer, Dorothy Belle Feiner was both beautiful and wealthy. The self-made groom effortlessly treated his bride to a sojourn in England. "A honeymoon trip to Europe would be the least one could expect from a young husband with the income of a Richard Rodgers," observes biographer Meryle Secrest. "One family story has it that that when he got married at the age of 27, he was making $75,000 a year"—this in 1930, when the depression was ravaging the country.

When Richard and Dorothy returned to Manhattan, she was pregnant, and he was preparing to head west with Hart: Paramount Studios had made the writers an offer they couldn't refuse. The Rodgers's first child, Mary, was born in 1931, and for the next four years the young family split their time between Beverly Hills and New York, with Richard staying mostly in Hollywood away from the family, working on films that never seemed to get made.

But one outstanding movie did find its way to the screen. There had been nothing like *Love Me Tonight* before; there's been nothing like it since. The film's opening number, sung by Maurice Chevalier and a large cast, features Hart's characteristic rhymed couplets. As the Parisian day begins, Rodgers's melody is irresistible, and everyone has his say in words or syllables that sweep viewers along:

TAXI DRIVER: *Isn't it romantic?*
Da, da, da, da, da,
And now sir we are here.
COMPOSER: *How much do I owe you?*
Da, da, da, da, da
TAXI DRIVER: *Two francs.*
COMPOSER: *Oh, that's too dear!*

[Cut to train compartment.]
Isn't it romantic?
Da, da, da, da, da
I'll write some words as well.
Isn't it romantic
Sitting on the train?
This song has got to sell!
[French soldiers on the train listen as he writes.]
While bravely at the throttle sits the engineer!

1ST SOLDIER: *Hey Henri, pass the bottle!*
2ND SOLDIER: *This is rotten beer!*
COMPOSER: *Isn't it romantic?*
Speeding right along
The outskirts of Paree!
SOLDIERS: *Isn't it romantic?*
Listen to that song!

1ST SOLDIER: *It's too damn long for me!*
SOLDIERS: *Da, da, da, da, da, da, da!*
We would rather sing than fight for France!
Isn't it romance?

When he wasn't working with Hart on film scores, Rodgers, joined by Dorothy, attended innumerable Beverly Hills dinner parties, only to find there was no escaping studio life. The routine proved as ritualized as a Noh play: the meal finished, the host—usually a film industry bigwig—would invite his guests into his living room. On his command, a wall would swing out, revealing a screen (without disturbing the Impressionist paintings). The dinner guests would then watch a forthcoming movie. "You never dared to express an opinion," Dorothy recalled, "because you never knew who was sitting next to you."

Love Me Tonight proved to be the pinnacle of Rodgers and Hart's cinematic career. They did some good film work for Al Jolson: *Hallelujah, I'm a Bum*, written in 1933, contained several outstanding songs, including "You Are Too Beautiful." And grinding out songs for MGM, they came up with "Easy to Remember," crooned by Bing Crosby in *Mississippi*. But for the most part their efforts fizzled.

Hart ran into the most difficulty. Studio heads found the Rodgers melodies acceptable but frequently sent Hart back to rewrite his lyrics. On one occasion only, this rewriting worked in Hart's favor. "Prayer" employed a simple lyric, intended for a Jean Harlow turn in *Hollywood Party*:

Oh, Lord
If you ain't busy up there,
I ask for help with a prayer
So please don't give me the air.

Neither Harlow nor "Prayer" appeared in the picture. Rodgers and Hart then adapted the song as the title number for *Manhattan Melodrama*. This time it had a different rhyme scheme:

Act One:
You gulp your coffee and run;
Into the subway you crowd.
Don't breathe, it isn't allowed.

The song again didn't make the cut. But it reappeared with a third set of lyrics, and this time it *did* make it into *Manhattan Melodrama*. Retitled "The Bad in Every Man," the song became a showstopper for nightclub chanteuse Shirley Ross:

Oh, Lord . . . .
I could be good to a lover,
But then I always discover
The bad in ev'ry man.

Hollywood legend has it that Hart ran into MGM's music publisher Jack Robbins after the film opened. Robbins remained ambivalent about the song: "You know, Larry, that's a really good tune you boys have there. I'd be glad to get behind it, but it needs a commercial lyric." Replied Hart, "Oh, yeah, I suppose what you'd like me to write is something corny, like 'blue moon.'" Robbins nodded, and Hart, for the first and last time, rewrote the song to please an executive:

Blue moon
You saw me standing alone,
Without a dream in my heart,
Without a love of my own.

"Blue Moon" became a phenomenal seller. But their Hollywood hit song proved Rodgers and Hart's Hollywood swan song.

Weary and disappointed, the men bought one-way tickets back to New York. Historian Ethan Mordden notes that cinema "wasn't a good form for them—though Hart had a terrific time. He loved the nightlife. He never really was much for working." As for Rodgers, he "so loved the theater he felt very fish out of water."

As the team waited out the final weeks of their contract, Richard wrote Dorothy about a worrying development. "I've experienced something I've never known before," he explained. "I have an active and intense feeling of depression which is absolutely impossible to shake off." One trigger for his black mood might well have been a *Los Angeles Examiner* column: "Whatever happened to Rodgers and Hart?" And then there was the farewell with Irving Thalberg. Wanting to thank the MGM production chief, who had first enticed him to Hollywood, Rodgers drove to the mogul's office, waited for a long stretch, and then was shown in. "Thalberg looked up with an uncomprehending, glassy look on his boyish face," the composer later wrote, "and I suddenly realized he hadn't the faintest idea who I was." Concluded Rodgers: "The studio might have lulled us into staying out there longer. But that would have been the end of Larry Hart and Dick Rodgers. I'm sure I would have ended up as a neurotic, a drunkard, or both." Tragically, he would wind up as both in his beloved New York.

Back in Gotham, he battled depression for about a year while he and Hart searched for the right vehicle to show audiences they were back in town. They found it in *Jumbo*, impresario Billy Rose's extravaganza. Staged in the mammoth New York Hippodrome, the musical, built around a circus, starred Jimmy Durante as a comic schemer stealing a pachyderm—until the cops catch him in the act. Thereupon he uttered the year's most famous line: "*What* elephant?" With *Jumbo*, Rodgers quietly established himself as America's Waltz King, with "Over and Over Again" and "The Most

Beautiful Girl in the World," displacing the Strausses, who had ruled the genre with their cloying hint of *Sacher torte mit schlag*. Rodgers injected an American verve and comic bounce, and music in three-quarter time would never be the same.

The show was the smash of 1935—the year Rodgers became a father again, of another daughter, Linda. He promised reporters that R & H would soon break new ground. He was right. Opening in April 1937, *Babes in Arms* made stars of complete unknowns—and featured some of Rodgers and Hart's most charming, sophisticated songs: "Where or When," "My Funny Valentine," "The Lady Is a Tramp," and "I Wish I Were in Love Again," with Hart's inimitable cascade:

The furtive sigh,
The blackened eye,
The words, "I'll love you 'til the day I die,"
The self-deception that believes the lie—
I wish I were in love again.

When love congeals
It soon reveals
The faint aroma of performing seals,
The double-crossing of a pair of heels.
I wish I were in love again!

In November of that year came *I'd Rather Be Right*. Starring George M. Cohan, this production audaciously satirized Franklin D. Roosevelt, the most popular president in American history. The following season R & H presented *The Boys from Syracuse* (with the great waltz "Falling in Love with Love"), the first Broadway musical based on Shakespearean comedy.

Hart hit the bottle so hard that he proved difficult to work with—when he didn't just up and disappear. With a deadline looming, Rodgers persuaded his partner to check into Doctors Hospital—and moved in with him, notebooks, piano, and all, so that they could compose while Larry dried out. The cure worked well enough to get the work done.

Then Hart backslid: he failed to appear at meetings, ignored his personal appearance, struggled with rhymes that once came effortlessly. There were still triumphs, like *Too Many Girls*, starring an unknown named Desi Arnaz, and *Pal Joey*, the first musical that dared to have an anti-hero, a heel played by Gene Kelly. By 1940, however, the partnership was in deep trouble.

Rodgers began to consider writing with another lyricist. Oscar Hammerstein II was the logical choice. The scion of a theatrical family—his uncle a noted Broadway producer and his father the Victoria Theater's manager—Hammerstein had written important shows with Vincent Youmans, Rudolf Friml, Sigmund Romberg, and Jerome Kern. But his last hit had been *Showboat*, way back in 1927. After a string of flops, he desperately sought the right collaborator. He and Rodgers, though not close friends, had known each other since their college days; they respected each other's work and occasionally lunched together.

Rodgers set up a meeting with Hammerstein to talk about Lynn Riggs's play *Green Grow the Lilacs*. The Theater Guild had just bought the rights, and Rodgers thought a creative musician and lyricist team could . . . Hammerstein didn't want to talk about it. Intrigued as he was, he warned, "It would kill Larry if you walked away while he was still able to function." Still, he added, "If the time ever comes when he cannot function, call me."

Alas, the time wasn't long in arriving. Larry expressed no interest in working on a "cowboy musical"—the adaptation of *Lilacs* that eventually became *Oklahoma!* Besides, he wanted to take a vacation in Mexico and then concentrate on a revival of *A Connecti-*

cut Yankee, an old Rodgers and Hart chestnut. Although Richard grumbled privately that there ought to be "a statute of limitations on gratitude," he nevertheless ponied up $100,000 to produce *Yankee*: he thought he owed it to Larry. Then he went to work with Oscar on the cowboy musical.

The difference between Hart and Hammerstein was the difference between klieg light and daylight. Oscar was a devoted family man, knowledgeable about the America that lay beyond New York City, instantly accessible, disciplined by habit, and optimistic by nature ("I just can't write anything without hope in it," he noted). Research was as key to Hammerstein's method as inspiration. For one song, he originally wrote: "The corn is as high as a cow pony's eye." Then he strolled in a cornfield and found the stalks considerably higher. The cowpoke's folksy simile became "as high as an elephant's eye."

Hammerstein worked alone, at glacial pace, painstakingly fashioning phrases before submitting the whole lyric to the composer. Rodgers worried about his new partner's approach until Hammerstein drove from his Doylestown, Pennsylvania, farmhouse to Richard's summer place in Fairfield, Connecticut, with the lyrics to "Oh, What a Beautiful Mornin'" in hand. Rodgers scanned the opening line, "There's a bright golden haze on the meadow." "I was sick with joy," he recalled. "When you're given words like that you've got something to say musically. You'd really have to be made of cement not to spark to that." He came up with a melody ten minutes later. This fluency always astonished Hammerstein: "I work for two weeks on a lyric," he said, "and hours later Dick has done his half of the work."

Hammerstein exaggerated, though not by much. *Oklahoma!* took time to coalesce. But by mid-1943 it was ready to go, perfected even further by the work of choreographer Agnes de Mille.

Rodgers had always liked the idea of big-name choreographers working with his music: in 1937, George Balanchine, fresh from the Ballets Russes de Monte Carlo, had staged the jazzy "Slaughter on Tenth Avenue" for Rodgers and Hart's *On Your Toes*.

Oklahoma! was a *coup de théâtre*—it ran for more than two thousand performances, made buckets of money, and changed the course of the American musical, integrating plot, songs, and dance in a new way. On Broadway there was now a different H in R & H, as critics duly noted.

Victory has a thousand fathers, but there was one orphan on *Oklahoma!*'s opening night, March 31, 1943. In the crush at Sardi's, a tiny figure broke through the crowd of adulators to tell Rodgers: "This show of yours will run forever." It was a generous remark by a man who must have been suffering deep psychological pain. Even though he and his partner still planned to write a few new songs for the Yankee revival, it was obvious that the Hart had gone out of the relationship.

Eight months later A *Connecticut Yankee* opened at the Martin Beck Theater. Larry showed up drunk, loudly singing along with the principals. Richard had him escorted out as the lilting melody and bright verse of the team's last black-humor song went on:

I married many men, a ton of them,
And yet I was untrue to none of them,
Because I bumped off every one of them
To keep my love alive. . . .

Sir Athelstane indulged in fratricide,
He killed his dad and that was patricide,
One night I stabbed him at my mattress side
To keep my love alive
To keep my love alive.

The next day Hart disappeared. Composer Fritz Loewe (*My Fair Lady*) found him the following night sitting on a curb on Eighth Avenue—drunk, feverish, and indifferent to the cold autumn rain. Loewe rushed Hart to Doctors Hospital and there, on November 22, he died, aged forty-eight. The official cause of death: pneumonia. It would have been truer to say that the lyricist died of self-inflicted wounds.

Objectively there was no reason for Rodgers to feel guilty: he had done all he could to save Larry from Larry. But while he threw himself into new projects with Hammerstein, subtle changes in the composer's mien spoke volumes. He began to look older than his years, heavier in the midsection, more lined in the face. His marriage suffered. He and Dorothy went on as a couple, but both daughters noted ominous silences and other signs of marital strain.

Stephen Sondheim, a Hammerstein acolyte, remembered Rodgers in the mid-1940s as he worked with Oscar to transform the Ferenc Molnár play *Liliom* into *Carousel*. Rodgers crafted some of his most beautiful and upbeat melodies for that show, yet he impressed the youthful Sondheim as discontented, acrimonious, and restive. The reason seemed obvious to Sondheim. When Rodgers worked with Hart, he was the responsible partner; with Hammerstein the roles had reversed. Hammerstein "was a generous, big-hearted man who devoted himself to good works such as the World Federalists and all those things," Sondheim observed. "He was more than just a book or lyric writer. He was a man of the theater. I suspect that Dick began to believe Oscar was seen this way and he was the mean little man in the office . . . the drunk. He became a whole other person."

Rodgers went public with his phobias. He expressed his fear of flying, of driving in tunnels and over bridges. And some part of him seemed to close down. He was now drinking to excess (sometimes as much as a bottle of vodka per diem), though few outside his family noticed—unlike Hart, he could hold his liquor. He didn't weave or slur his words; he simply became more withdrawn. Even when sober, Rodgers found social occasions increasingly a strain. Hammerstein's son, William, lunched several times with Rodgers and found his host enigmatic. "I was never comfortable with him, and I mentioned this to Dad," he recalled. Oscar replied, "Nobody is. It's not you, it's Dick."

Yet the soaring melodies still poured forth—even richer and more complex. Lorenz Hart brought out Rodgers's glittering surface; Oscar Hammerstein probed deeper, forcing his collaborator to write more serious and sustained melodies. In Molnár's *Liliom*, for example, the lovers exchange two lines:

> LILIOM: *But you wouldn't marry a rough guy like me—that is—eh—if you loved me.*
> JULIE: *Yes, I would—if I loved you, Mr. Liliom.*

For *Carousel*, Hammerstein switched the locale from France to New England and used their words as the springboard entirely expressed in the conditional:

> *If I loved you,*
> *Time and again I would try to say*
> *All I'd want you to know.*
> *If I loved you,*
> *Words wouldn't come in an easy way—*
> *Round in circles I'd go!*
> *Longin' to tell you, but afraid and shy,*
> *I'd let my golden chances pass me by.*
> *Soon you'd leave me,*
> *Off you would go in the mist of day,*
> *Never, never to know*

How I loved you—
If I loved you.

Rodgers's tune captures the poignancy and sexual tension of the lovers. That song, along with "June Is Bustin' Out All Over" and other powerhouse numbers, made *Carousel* the most talked-about musical of 1945. One song, "You'll Never Walk Alone," perfectly captured the renewed faith and optimism of postwar America:

When you walk through a storm,
Hold your head up high
And don't be afraid of the dark.
At the end of the storm
Is a golden sky
And the sweet silver song of a lark.

Rodgers and Hammerstein were not infallible. They stubbed their toes with *Pipe Dream*, adapted from John Steinbeck's raffish *Cannery Row*, and with the backstage story *Me and Juliet*, their only show not based on a book or straight play. Still, they remained Broadway royalty.

It was during *Juliet* rehearsals in 1955 that Rodgers felt twinges of pain in his left jaw. X-rays showed a malignant growth. "He was very fearful about health," his daughter Mary said. "When he finally got cancer of the jaw I think he was relieved, because he'd been waiting for something to happen for so long when it finally happened it was like, 'Oh, well, now I've got *that* over with.'"

Doctors removed part of Rodgers's jaw and all the teeth from the cancerous side of his mouth. The procedure would have sidelined other patients for months. Ten days later Rodgers was tending to rehearsals. That *Juliet* had a disappointingly short run hardly mattered. What *was* vital was the next show, and the show after that. No one in the family (or out of it, for that matter) had ever seen the composer sit at the piano and play for sheer enjoyment. He only went to the ivories to write a song for a specific character in a specific musical. It was all he knew how to do, all he wanted to do. He had no close friends, no hobbies, no wish to visit foreign climes. Broadway was his life.

Partly this was due to his half-alcoholic/half-workaholic nature, partly because he found his marriage confining. He needed Dorothy and relied on her judgment about theatrical matters. She was a strong-minded, capable woman, who had run a business that maintained high-end apartments. In her spare time she had invented the Jonny Mop, a toilet-cleaning device that, to her amusement, became a department store best-seller. But she was also a compulsive manager, at once a boon and a trial for her husband. According to their daughter Linda, "It was a strange relationship. They needed and supported each other, and were the worst people in the world for each other. When he had problems she was always there to take charge. I am not sure he had much of a say. He was quite a passive partner."

To escape, Rodgers fled to the theater whenever possible, taking comfort in aspects of show business that everyone else loathed: the out-of-town tryouts, the frantic rewrites, even the delicatessen sandwiches and pickles that are the cuisine of showfolk in rehearsal. And he became inordinately fond of various chorines and divas. "He liked to talk about all the young ladies of the stage he had known," says Shirley Jones in *The Sweetest Sounds*, a PBS documentary about Rodgers. "He called them his little friends, so obviously he had quite a few romances." But the dalliances did not relieve a persistent malaise, a feeling of inadequacy he could never quite define. Alcohol could not assuage it, nor could the five psychiatrists he consulted.

Troubled he may have been, but the composer retained a clear head for business. In the 1950s he and Hammerstein became producers as well as writers, seeking to control the financial and aesthetic facets of every show. They had watched insensitive producers excise favorite numbers, and they resolved that it would never happen again. By the end of the decade they were an institution. No other Broadway team, past or present, had written so many influential stage musicals, with so many songs that had entered the American bloodstream.

From *South Pacific*, for example, had come "Some Enchanted Evening," "There Is Nothing Like a Dame," "Younger Than Springtime"—and the achingly self-conscious editorial, "You've Got to Be Carefully Taught":

You've got to be taught to be afraid
Of people whose eyes are oddly made,
And people whose skin is a different shade
You've got to be carefully taught.
You've got to be taught before it's too late
Before you are six or seven or eight,
To hate all the people your relatives hate,
You've got to be carefully taught.

No one could accuse Rodgers and Hammerstein of hypocrisy. The duo's supreme achievement was 1951's *The King and I*, with its pageant of unforgettable songs, including "Whistle a Happy Tune" and "Shall We Dance?" Brilliantly directed by choreographer Jerome Robbins, the show presented a candid view of people whose eyes were "oddly made"—the court of nineteenth-century Siam, with its complicated monarch, his intimidated wives, and the forthright English governess whose encounter with the king presents the greatest unconsummated love story in the annals of musical theater. The team returned to Asian themes in *Flower Drum Song*, about Chinese Americans in San Francisco. This too had best-selling numbers, including "I Enjoy Being a Girl."

Alas, at the end of the decade, the second R & H partnership came to a tragic end: doctors diagnosed Oscar with terminal stomach cancer. *The Sound of Music*, the duo's final show, opened at the Lunt-Fontanne Theater in 1959. The *Herald Tribune* review expressed the lukewarm critical reaction: "Not only too sweet for words, but almost too sweet for music." It didn't matter. Rodgers and Hammerstein's finale ran for 1,443 performances, the 1965 film version was an even bigger grosser, and several of the songs, notably, "Do-Re-Mi," "Edelweiss," and "My Favorite Things" became pop classics. Those who found the last song saccharine were in for a surprise when they heard jazz saxophonist John Coltrane's evocative version. They had forgotten that Rodgers never let himself be pigeonholed. Call his music impertinent, and he'd come up with something serious; accuse him of sliding backward to operetta, and he would write a song to challenge the hippest jazzman.

Oscar Hammerstein II died on August 23, 1960, aged sixty-five. Rodgers was devastated. He was only fifty-eight, unready "to be turned out to pasture." Rodgers added: "It's very easy for an upset man to retire. As you get older you get more scared. But what would I do if I retired? I'm not a golfer." He had worked with two collaborators over a forty-three-year career, and it would not be easy to find another. His talent for luck had begun to run out.

While he pondered the possibilities, the Rodgers family settled into apartments at the Hotel Pierre. There Richard became his own wordsmith, writing the lyrics as well as the melodies of *No Strings*, a groundbreaking story of an interracial romance. The rhymes had neither the jounce of Hart nor the sentiment of Hammerstein, but the title song became a cabaret standard:

The sweetest sounds I'll ever hear
Are still inside my head.
The kindest words I'll ever know
Are waiting to be said.

Rodgers never flew solo again. Asocial as he could be, the consummate music man needed company. He worked with the prominent (Sondheim in *Do I Hear a Waltz?* and Sheldon Harnick in *Rex*) as well as the uncelebrated (Martin Charnin in *Two by Two* and *I Remember Mama*). Yet though his work was never less than creditable, he had passed his prime.

During Rodgers's decline, the afflictions he had feared in Hollywood roared back. He wound up in the hospital, suffering from alcoholism and depression. Then cancer returned in his seventy-second year, this time in his throat. He underwent a laryngectomy, depriving him of his normal voice and forcing him to learn esophageal speech. Observed Rodgers's daughter Linda, "For somebody who gave such incredible pleasure to so many millions of people, not to have had the same kind of joy and contentment and comfort in his own life—is just awful."

He went on searching for new refrains until his death on December 30, 1979, at the Pierre. His body was cremated. There is no grave, no statue, no marker; the location of his ashes is a secret.

As, finally, is the musician himself. What had troubled him from the early days has never definitively become clear. But one clue shows up in the last words of his autobiography, *Musical Stages*. "There is a traditional trick," he writes, "that theater people have played as long as I can remember. A veteran member of a company will order a gullible newcomer to find the key to the curtain. Naturally, the joke is that there is no such thing. I have been in the theater over fifty years, and I don't think anyone would consider me naive, but all my life I've been searching for that key."

If that key remained undiscovered, he found all the other keys, from C to shining C. The notes he put together over a lifetime make him a pantheon figure in American music—indeed in world music—beyond time and fashion. That his mystery endures matters little beside his sweet, ever-enduring melodies.

Sondheim vs. Sondheim

Only a handful of major Broadway composers have written lyrics to accompany their own melodies: Irving Berlin, Noel Coward, Jerry Herman, Cole Porter, and Stephen Sondheim. Of that extraordinary group, Sondheim enjoys the highest critical status. He has earned clutches of Tonys, a Grammy, an Oscar, the Kennedy Center and British Olivier Awards, and a Pulitzer Prize. Doctoral students study his compositions; he is a favorite of newspaper theater sections here and abroad; a quarterly magazine, *The Sondheim Review*, prints nothing but examinations of, and interviews with, the Master; and every year or so there is either a new Sondheim show or a revival of one of his past works. And still the writer ruefully observes, "I've never been popular."

That's not bogus self-deprecation. Sondheim's musical *Assassins* opened in 2004 to admiring reviews—and slammed shut after two months. A string of other Sondheim shows have had early closures and unprofitable runs, among them *Anyone Can Whistle* (1964), *Follies* (1971), *Pacific Overtures* (1976), *Merrily We Roll Along* (1981), and *Passion* (1994).

Sondheim's history of flops has been one of Broadway's greatest conundrums for almost half a century: why should an artist who inspires such intense devotion be so resistible to so many theatergoers? Is it because he crams his lyrics with complex rhyme schemes and unexpected feints and thrusts? There can be no better example of this than the work he did for *A Little Night Music.* The musical was based on Ingmar Bergman's 1956 dark comedy, *Smiles of a Summer Night.* The film director/scenarist recalled, "I felt it would be a technical challenge to make a comedy with a mathematical pattern—man/woman, man/woman. Four couples. And then muddle them up and sort out the equations." This was just the sort of problem that Sondheim loved to solve. He wrote "character songs" defining the amorous conflicts of various personae—and containing such unexpected rhymes that they seemed to astonish the singers as they mouthed them:

No, no, not even figs—raisins.
Ah, liaisons.

But "Liaisons" is only one aspect of Sondheim's work. He can also write simple gags with the rhythm of a metronome, as in the tyrant's braggadocio for *A Funny Thing Happened on the Way to the Forum.* Miles Gloriosus, literally "boastful soldier" in Latin, is a stock comic character used to great effect by the Roman playwright Plautus. Sondheim captures Plautus's spirit in a cascade of braggadocio. The officer describes himself as admired/inspired/desired and caps these with a flattering appraisal of his own appearance:

In dress the best displayed,
I am a parade!

Have theatergoers stayed away because Sondheim's melodies can be as elusive as anything Leonard Bernstein ever wrote? Yet he can also compose tunes that a stone could hum: "Send in the Clowns," for example, a melody heard in elevators and restaurants around the world.

It's not an on-again-off-again talent that explains Sondheim's strange duality. Instead the evidence suggests that there are two Sondheims, a mainstream artist and a contrarian, with a willfully perverse wish *not* to appeal to the general public. That second Sondheim has been in the ascendant for many years.

Starting with *West Side Story*, his Broadway debut as a wordsmith (Bernstein wrote the music), Sondheim displayed a gift for seizing an idea and giving it wings. Take the number "Gee, Officer Krupke." Before anyone had coined the term "political correctness," at a time when the idea of "root causes" only applied to diseased agriculture, a group of young malefactors mocked the juvenile courts that they blatantly abused. At the time, Sondheim and his collaborators were keenly aware of the hypocrisies of the social work establishment, the uses of excuses, the evaporation of personal responsibility, the all too frequent turn-'em-loose policies of the criminal court system that ascribed all sorts of offenses to "root causes" (even though most of the wrongdoers' peers had the same background and lived decent lives).

This, of course, was before Leonard Bernstein hosted a notorious party for the Black Panthers, much mocked by Tom Wolfe in his wry exposé *Radical Chic*. And before the romanticizing of prison inmates by Norman Mailer, who made an icon of the murderer Jack Henry Abbott by declaring "culture is worth a risk," only to see that risk pay horrific dividends when the new parolee stabbed a waiter to death after a minor dispute.

In the 1950s it was still acceptable, even among those who would later become the chic-est of the chic, to tell the truth about life in the city. Ergo, Bernstein, book writer Arthur Laurents, and

Sondheim himself set up a mock court hearing onstage. Various youths address an imaginary judge. No misdeed has ever been the fault of the soloist. Each offers an exculpatory excuse. One has parents who smoke marijuana but won't share the weed with the kids. Another might have been aborted, but somehow the procedure didn't take. A third is violent because his father abuses his mother and she abuses him. Another has an alcoholic grandfather, a drug-pushing grandmother, a sister who wears a mustache. The capper:

My brother wears a dress
Goodness, gracious, that's why I'm a mess!

This number, deriding the fakery of the street-smart wise guys and exposing the emerging social-work and psychiatric no-fault orthodoxy, was remarkably prescient. Bernstein, who later personified radical chic in his support of the Black Panthers, would never return to the attitude of "Krupke." And Sondheim edged away from it too, until he seemed to embrace what he once ridiculed.

The lyricist was just twenty-seven when *West Side Story* opened to acclaim in the fall of 1957. Critics hailed Sondheim as a Broadway *wunderkind*. In the *Journal-American*, John McClain spoke for most of the aisle-sitters: "Young Mr. Sondheim has gone all the way with the mood in his lyrics. His ballads are the lament of the sincere, and he can come up with the most hilarious travesty of our times—'Gee, Officer Krupke'—a plaint which should settle the problem of juvenile delinquency forever."

In 1957, Bernstein was one of America's foremost conductors and composers; director Jerome Robbins had established himself as one of the nation's most imaginative choreographers; and the book writer, Arthur Laurents, was a much produced playwright and scenarist. But who was this kid, this total unknown? Sondheim's astonishing arrival seemed a melodramatic *deus ex machina*. In fact, like most overnight discoveries, he had served a long and rigorous apprenticeship.

The only child of affluent dress manufacturer Herbert Sondheim, Stephen grew up in Manhattan until the age of ten. Then, in 1940, his parents divorced and his world went into reverse. He had to transfer from a comfortable New York school to a military academy. Home also changed, from a city apartment to a large country house in Bucks County, Pennsylvania, where the boy lived with his mother, Janet Fox Sondheim, known as "Foxy."

After the split, Foxy became possessive and overbearing, casting her son as an emotional stand-in for his absent father. In Meryle Secrest's biography *Stephen Sondheim: A Life*, the subject speaks about his mother in the years following the divorce: "She would hold my hand in theaters. . . . I remember going to a play with her and she not only held my hand, but looked at me during the entire play. It was really upsetting." Then he became aware that she was trying to seduce him. "Well, she would sit across from me with her legs aspread. She would lower her blouse and that sort of stuff. . . . When my father left her, she substituted me for him. And she used me the way she had used him, to come on to and to berate, beat up on, you see. What she did for five years was treat me like dirt, but come on to me at the same time."

Thus began a strange, sorry-grateful relationship that would play out over a conflicted adolescence and young manhood. On the one hand, Stephen found himself severely discomfited by his mother's possessive and celebrity-collecting lifestyle. References to Foxy appeared in many a Sondheim song over the years, none more acrimonious than "The Ladies Who Lunch," describing wealthy women of a certain age. Looking back on his childhood, Sondheim once remarked that he felt nothing special about his parents' divorce. "The world is full of mothers and fathers like mine. It's just that my mother was an extreme case." But then he added that "Foxy" Sondheim was a pretentious and compulsive liar—and that "her values were, to put it mildly, askew. She only really cared about celebrity and money." He made no attempt to disguise his revulsion; Mary Rodgers, the daughter of Richard Rodgers, and one of Stephen's closest friends, sent him a gift. He wrote a warm note, ending, "Thank-you for the plate, but where was my mother's head?" Clearly "Foxy" was just the sort of person he had in mind when he wrote the song about a woman with a surfeit of money and a dearth of direction, filling her days with plans for brunches on her own behalf, running to the gym, trying on new outfits she doesn't need, and breaking bread with others of her ilk. What made the song so remarkable, aside from Elaine Stritch's acute rendering, was the fact that it seemed to have been written from the inside. The writer was not merely observing the lady who lunched, he *was* the lady who lunched. His secret: "The way you get into character—the way you get in the song, both musically and lyrically—is to become the character. It's the only way. I don't know how else you do it, unless you're the playwright who created the character in the first place. But I'm always writing for characters that somebody else has created." Not always. Not here. Not with

A toast to that invincible bunch,
The dinosaurs surviving the crunch.

Yet he owed a great deal to one member of his mother's bunch—Oscar Hammerstein II. Her Bucks County neighbor provided the most important creative influence in Stephen's career. In early adolescence Sondheim befriended Oscar's son, Jimmy, and began hanging around the Hammerstein house. When the Broadway pro learned that his young visitor wanted to write musicals, he offered avuncular encouragement and advice.

At fifteen, Stephen thought he was ready for the Big Time. He composed a score for his school musical and showed it to Oscar. In *Sondheim & Co.*, biographer Craig Zadan quotes Stephen's account of that epochal meeting: "He said, 'Now you want my opinion as though I didn't really know you? Well, it's the worst thing I've ever read.'" As the youth's lower lip trembled, Oscar went on: "Now, I didn't say that it was untalented, I said it was terrible. And if you want to know why it was terrible, I'll tell you."

Hammerstein proceeded to rip apart every detail, from stage directions to rhymes. Recalled Sondheim, "At the risk of hyperbole, I'd say in that afternoon I learned more about songwriting and the musical theater than most people learn in a lifetime." Never did the man talk down to the boy. Slowly, deliberately, Oscar spoke of structure and the value of each word; how essential simplicity was; how to introduce character; the interrelationship of music and rhyme. "He was at least as good a critic as he was a writer. Most people think of Oscar as a kind of affable, idealistic lunkhead. Instead, he was a very sophisticated, sharp-tongued, articulate man," Sondheim noted.

Over the next few years Hammerstein encouraged and instructed as Sondheim worked on various experiments, from a musical adaptation of the old George S. Kaufman–Marc Connelly comedy *Beggar on Horseback* to an adaptation of a serious play, Maxwell Anderson's *High Tor*. None reached the public, but all were stepping-stones to Broadway.

At Williams College, Sondheim majored in music and worked on the score for an original musical called *Saturday Night*. Upon graduation he won a two-year fellowship to study with avant-garde composer Milton Babbitt in New York. Babbitt remembered him well: "No one could have been more serious about his music than Steve. . . . He wanted his music to be as sophisticated and as knowing within the obvious restraints of a Broadway musical." Despite grandiose plans, *Saturday Night* proved another dead-end exercise. But the songs made ideal audition numbers for prospective backers. Sondheim's name soon got around at showbiz parties. To the cognoscenti, he became known as the best unknown songwriter in town.

That label wasn't to last much longer. Sondheim's work drew Bernstein's attention. The great musician wanted the young man to co-write *West Side Story*'s lyrics. Working with a big name enticed Sondheim, but he held back. He considered himself primarily a musician, and he hated to share credit with anyone—even Lenny. What's more, he thought the material was beyond his experience. "I can't do this show," he told his agent. "I've never been that poor, and I've never even *known* a Puerto Rican!" Advised that this was a story of star-crossed lovers, not a sociological treatise, he sighed like a prisoner and wrote like an angel. The rewards were a little fame, a lot of money, and his first movie sale.

Sondheim intended to make his next Broadway work a solo job, but it wasn't to be. An opportunity came up to work with Jule Styne on the *ur*–show business musical *Gypsy*, and Sondheim grabbed it. Styne's brash melodies established the theme, and Sondheim amplified it. He was just beginning a lyrical style that was to mature and sharpen when he started writing his own tunes, allowing a good deal more freedom than he had when marrying lyrics to someone else's notes, no matter how gifted that someone was. His technique for *Gypsy* added an element of surprise to the wit, rhyming "he goes" and "she goes," then adding two punch lines:

No fits, no fights, no feuds and no egos,
Amigos,
Together!

Gypsy starred Ethel Merman as the adrenal mother of stripper Gypsy Rose Lee and her sister, June Havoc. She was precisely the kind of woman Sondheim knew in his bones. He caught her psyche in the classic "Some People":

Some people sit on their butts,
Got the dream, yeah, but not the guts.

In a rare self-appraisal, Merman said she had "a distinctive voice, a lot of boldness and no heart." Such, in any case, was her version of *Gypsy*'s monstrous stage mother. When the diva added, "Broadway has been good to me, but then, I've been good to Broadway," no one disagreed.

Gypsy was another smash, annihilating any fears of a sophomore jinx and propelling Sondheim to his primary goal: writing words and music for a major musical comedy. *A Funny Thing Happened on the Way to the Forum* was the writer's true proving ground. For even with the explosively comic Zero Mostel, the Roman farce bombed out of town; no one in the audience seemed to know what the show was about. After all, the plot was a jumble of knockabout farceurs in and out of complicated troubles—all taking place in ancient Rome. There, slaves try manfully (and sometimes womanfully) to gain their freedom by hook or by crook. In the case of one called Pseudolus, it is preferably by crook. His owner is a handsome youth named Hero, and this worthy is in love with the beautiful Philia, who works in the brothel next door. Hero promises Pseudolus his freedom—if he will help him win Philia's heart. There's just one hitch to all this: the courtesan is already engaged to Miles Gloriosus. Philia and Hero do fall in love, but all sorts of subterfuges and disguises are necessary before they can wed, including a grand *deus ex machina* at the end, in which it is revealed that Hero and Miles are actually brother and sister. The boastful soldier is not a fan of incest and thus is willing to forsake the girl and return to the wars. All this was explained in "Comedy Tonight," crafted over a weekend in Washington, D.C., where *Forum* was trying out. It provided a billboard in rhyme. Example:

Tumblers! Fumblers! Grumblers! Mumblers!
No royal curse, no Trojan horse,
And a happy ending of course!

The song, letting the audience know that they were about to see a knockdown farce set to music, turned fortunes around. *Forum* opened at the Alvin Theater in May 1968 and ran for 964 performances—a longer Broadway run than *West Side Story*, than *Gypsy*, than any subsequent Sondheim show.

Now that it was clear that Sondheim was no fluke, he began to generate his own productions. This was no downhill slalom. The second time out on his own, Sondheim came up with *Anyone Can Whistle*, starring Angela Lansbury. A few songs had distinction, but Arthur Laurents's staging was so chaotic and campy that audiences began walking out during the first act. Nine performances later, it closed.

Sondheim described *Anyone Can Whistle* as "a sort of music student's score. That whole score is based on the opening four notes of the overture, which is a second going to a fourth. All the songs are based on seconds and fourths and the relationship between a D and an E and a C and an F." But as usual with the composer, he left a number of things unsaid. In fact Sondheim, then in the middle of intensive psychoanalysis, was coming to grips not only with his long-suppressed homosexuality but also with his distrust of emotional intimacy. Tony Walton, who designed the show's sets and costumes, recalled Stephen singing the title number, the lament of a woman yearning to express her emotions, reflecting that what seems hard might actually be simple, that being natural was what was hard:

Maybe you could show me
How to let go
Lower my guard.

Sondheim's rendition "seemed so autobiographical," Walton observed. "It made me think of Noel Coward on his seventieth birthday, singing, 'All I've had is a talent to amuse.'" Arthur Laurents agreed: "I always thought that song would be Steve's epitaph."

After the closing, Sondheim unwisely decided to collaborate once more—this time with Broadway giant Richard Rodgers, whose partner, Oscar Hammerstein II, had recently died. Sondheim was wary, but he remembered saying to himself, "Okay, I'm doing my little obligation to Oscar, I'm going to make a lot of money, and it's an easy job."

Wrong on all counts. Hammerstein would probably have disdained to adapt Laurents's arch drama, *The Time of the Cuckoo*, about a loveless spinster in Rome. The show, never compelling to audiences, didn't have a hit in it and barely broke even. And working with Rodgers was a horror. The composer drank heavily and at one time bawled out his young collaborator in front of the whole company. Sondheim furiously exited but was talked into making peace with his collaborator. Sondheim said little at the time, though later he claimed that the show "deserved to fail." Rodgers would describe Sondheim as someone whom he watched "grow from an attractive little boy to a monster."

Until now Sondheim had worked within established traditions; *Company* changed all that. The composer had all-new partners: Harold Prince as producer, Michael Bennett as director, George Furth as book writer. The musical broke with tradition: there was no chorus and precious little plot. There was also a rare and daring sophistication. *Company* debuted during the Age of Aquarius, when cutting-edge Broadway fare emphasized nudity and single entendres. At a time when shows like *Oh! Calcutta!* and *Hair* were getting all the ink, *Company* went its own singular and intellectually demanding way. In a canny review of a recent *Company* revival, the gay magazine *Advocate* noted: "The musical revolves around Bobby's 35th birthday party and his relationships with four married couples and three women he's dating, all of whom wonder when he's going to get married. This is a guy who isn't a kid anymore, who decorated his own apartment, who drinks heavily, who habitually deflects attention by asking questions, whose friends notice that he's always on the outside looking in, who beds women but never talks about commitment to anyone who isn't already married or otherwise clearly unavailable. . . . Hello?"

Nonetheless the original version had no intention of venturing out of the closet, or making any sort of declaration about civil rights or identity politics. Instead of probing for motivations, it went for a new kind of Broadway score. Happily, that score contained brilliant patter songs, some melodies that suggested Ravel at his most inventive, and a couple of ballads about wedded life, sung (and written) by a kind of psychological voyeur who thinks:

Good things get better,
Bad things get worse.
Wait, I think I meant that in reverse.

And a bride's charmingly terrified monologue to the assembled witnesses, "Getting Married Today" became an instant classic:

Look, perhaps
I'll collapse
In the apse.

Company's overtone, though, was decidedly anti-marriage. The singles and the couples seemed attractive to look at but not to know, and one number, "Little Things You Do Together," sung by a husband and wife, contained a cringe-making element of autobiography. It's the

Neighbors you annoy together
Children you destroy together
That keeps marriage intact.

The out-of-town tryout in Boston earned scattered commendations and one heavy brickbat from *Variety*: Sondheim's songs proved "undistinguished"; furthermore it was "evident that the author, George Furth, hates femmes and makes them all out to be conniving, cunning, cantankerous, and cute. . . . As it stands now, it's for ladies' matinees, homos, and misogynists." The New York critics were kinder and wiser; *Time* and *Newsweek* hailed *Company* as a "landmark" and "so brilliant it passes over one like a shock wave." In London, reviewers set the tone that was to greet almost every subsequent Sondheim work. The *Sunday Times* was typical: "There are no native composers in this city of the varied brilliance of Stephen Sondheim, who is responsible for both music and lyrics—lyrics that are sometimes sharp as an icicle, and that at others set the mind achingly dreaming of unforgotten joys and irrational sorrows."

Yet it was the *New York Times*'s influential Sunday critic, Walter Kerr, who kept his cool and made the most discerning comments.

After praising the cast, the direction, and Sondheim's "sophisticated and pertinacious" work, he concluded, "Now ask me if I liked the show. I didn't like it. I admired it. . . . Personally, I'm sorry-grateful."

This sort of ambiguous tribute would follow Sondheim for most of his career. Working with Prince again, but with various book writers, the composer/lyricist turned out five shows: *Follies* (written by James Goldman), *A Little Night Music* (Hugh Wheeler), *Pacific Overtures* (John Weidman), *Sweeney Todd* (Wheeler), and *Merrily We Roll Along* (Furth). No one could accuse Sondheim of a lack of originality—or of a yen for consistency. His work acquired a new polish, and his rhymes dug deep into character and history. His next show was *Follies*, a musical with an intriguing premise: life seen as a vaudeville program. Scene: a rundown Broadway theater. On its decrepit premises, a reunion takes place. The old-timers are former headliners of the Weisman Follies (read Ziegfeld Follies). The title is ambiguous: it refers to the careers of two show business couples, and it also concerns the miscalculations and missteps of their public careers and private lives.

Predictably, both couples have difficult marriages and act out (and dance out) their problems in assorted numbers. These often involve images of their younger selves when a different kind of entertainment sold tickets on the Great White Way. Many of the songs are clever pastiches of Tin Pan Alley in its heyday. "Losing My Mind," for example, was written in the melodic style of George Gershwin, with bright, Dorothy Fields–style lyrics; "The Story of Lucy and Jessie" echoed the saline approach of Cole Porter.

Yet *Follies* aimed higher than imitation and nostalgia. According to the composer/lyricist, the reason that book writer James Goldman chose vaudeville as metaphor was that "the Follies represented a state of mind of America between the two World Wars. Up until 1945, America was the good guy, everything was idealistic and hopeful and America was going to lead the world. Now you see the country is a riot of national guilt, the dream has collapsed, everything has turned to rubble underfoot, and that was what the show was about—the collapse of the dream."

In the early 1970s audiences weren't interested in editorials presented in Broadway musical form. They wanted "book" shows whose plots were easy to follow and whose songs they could hum. *Follies* lost its entire $800,000 investment, though it garnered seven Tonys and the Drama Critics Circle Award as the Best Musical of the Year.

In 1973 a group of singers offered a one-night tribute to the composer, featuring songs going back to *Saturday Night*. That event, coupled with the release of the original-cast album of *Follies*, prompted *New York Times* critic John S. Wilson to assess Sondheim's achievement. "He is, in effect, a summation and an elevation of all the lyric writing that has gone before him. To have this made clear in an evening's program of 40 songs covering 20 years is impressive. But to find this point being made with equal clarity in a single score is an indication of the creative level at which Sondheim has arrived."

"Arrived" was the operative word. Sondheim had now achieved the status of cult figure, and from here on, whatever he wrote enjoyed a respectful, if not downright awed, reception from a growing group of enthusiasts that included reviewers, cabaret singers, and non-showbiz "civilians" who made best-sellers of the original-cast recordings of his productions.

None of this seemed to affect the writer, at once gnawed by self-doubt and consumed by ambition. The British playwright Alan Ayckbourne remembered meeting Sondheim at an Oxford restaurant to discuss a possible project. "He speaks very, very fast and very, very quietly and he tends, certainly with people he doesn't know, to stare anywhere but at the person. I talk very, very fast and very, very quietly and don't stare at people either. So there were two guys—one of us could have left the table and the other would never have known it." Conversely Elaine Stritch, one of Sondheim's favorite performers, said, "He really lets you have it. He's terrible when you're not with it, but when you get it right he is so overjoyed by the material being interpreted the way he saw it that he makes you feel like a million bucks." And more than once, Jonathan Tunick saw the composer *willing* his material to thrive, "standing at the back of the house during a run-through or a tech rehearsal, his face bathed in tears."

To provide a little comic relief, Sondheim took time off in 1972 to write a mystery movie, *The Last of Sheila*, collaborating with actor Anthony Perkins. "Not having to write lyrics," said Stephen later, "made it like a vacation." This vigorous but rather nasty send-up of Agatha Christie, starring James Mason and Raquel Welch, displayed a few glints of wit but was "boy's work, not man's work," and he soon buckled down to write his next show.

A Little Night Music marked the return of the mainstream Sondheim. Laurents's book was a slyly commercial adaptation of *Smiles of a Summer Night*, Ingmar Bergman's peek at drawing-room and bedroom shenanigans in nineteenth-century Sweden. As a tribute to the epoch and the subject matter, Sondheim began thinking in terms of "fughettos, canons, contrapuntal duets, trios" and eventually composed every number in three-quarter time. The best of the waltzes, "Send in the Clowns," is the only Sondheim song to have reached the status of a platinum megahit, recorded by the likes of Sarah Vaughan, Frank Sinatra, and Judy Collins. More than thirty years later the bittersweet words still resound in the cabarets of Europe and America:

Finally finding the one that I wanted was yours.

Oddly enough, the song was written for the British actress Glynis Johns, who had a narrow vocal range. With her shortcoming in mind, Sondheim carefully wrote a number that scarcely stretched past an octave. Yet within this restricted format he created elusive musical and lyrical phrases that haunted theatergoers and, more significantly, musicians. Indeed, "Clowns" was to become more than a cabaret singer's favorite, it went on to be a new jazz standard.

In 1976, though, the contrarian Sondheim surfaced once more. *Pacific Overtures* told the story of nineteenth-century Japan's collision with Western influence. It was intellectually provocative and emotionally parched (193 performances; a loss of its entire $650,000 investment). *Sweeney Todd*, a tongue-in-cheek thriller about the partnership of a nineteenth-century London pie maker and a killer whose victims wind up in her creations, enjoyed a better reception. The opening number set the tone:

His skin was pale, and his eye was odd.

But not half so odd as the Little Barbershop of Horrors that followed. More than the bloody stage effects, it was Sondheim's haunting music that supplied the frissons. As the chorus encourages Sweeney to "Swing your razor wide," the melody echoes the notes of the *Dies Irae* (Day of Wrath), from the thirteenth-century Mass of the Dead. One character begins singing in a joyful major key; another takes up the tune, but in a minor version that gives a sense of foreboding. Meters constantly change, sometimes within a few bars, jumping from 4/4 to 2/4 to 5/4, indicating the instability of the main characters as well as the society in which they move and murder. "Those of us who write songs," Sondheim reflected, "should stage each number within an inch of its life in our own heads when we write." The director and choreographer "may not use anything in your blueprint at all, but they have something to work on, something to build from." In this case, the blueprint worked wonders.

Sweeney, with every piece of dialogue set to music, won eight Tonys, including Best Score, Best Book, Best Direction, and Best Musical. On opening night, drama critic Harold Clurman challenged Schuyler Chapin, the general manager of the Metropolitan Opera: "Why didn't you put this on at the Met?" Replied Chapin, "I would have put it on like a shot, if I'd had the opportunity." He added, "And I would have. There would have been screams and yells and I wouldn't have given a damn. Because it is an opera. A modern American opera." Bearing out Chapin's claim, revivals of *Sweeney Todd* later emphasized its Verdiesque qualities, particularly those performances at the New York City Opera and the Royal National Theatre in London.

Again the profits failed to arrive; the show earned back only 59 percent of its investment. But by now there was no shortage of producers willing to get involved with anything the composer chose to write. Sondheim had become synonymous with glamour; prestige belonged to anything with his name on it. Revivals began to open in regional theaters across the United States and Britain, and if the royalties from these productions were small, they eventually mounted up to more than $1 million a year for their creator, and more for those who had expressed financial faith in his efforts.

And then came *Merrily We Roll Along*. Preceding it was a minor heart attack that did little to slow Sondheim down. He quickly went to work on what seemed a standard Broadway adaptation of the Moss Hart–George S. Kaufman play. In this tragicomedy, lives and careers take place backward, starting with the corruption of success and winding up at an innocent high school graduation. The 1981 musical lasted just sixteen performances, triggering a breakup with Prince, who had produced and/or directed five consecutive Sondheim works.

For months the dejected writer holed up in his Turtle Bay townhouse, working on crossword puzzles and playing the board games that had always intrigued him—anything to take his mind away from public failure. "I am serious," he commented lugubriously, "but I'm serious in an art that is hardly worth being called one. There's a case to be made for 'Am I wasting my time in the long run?'" A friend recalled, "Steve was in a very dark place in his head and in his life. . . . It was bleak."

Sondheim's personal situation didn't improve his mood. He had friends in the entertainment business, but he lived alone; he had gone solo since college. Theater people knew he was gay; they also knew he was extremely private, and kept their distance. What only a few knew was the extent to which Foxy still pervaded his life. A few years before, she had entered the hospital to have a pacemaker installed. The night before the operation, she had a letter hand-delivered to her son, "because," said Stephen, "she thought she was going to die and wanted to make sure I got it." The note's bottom line: "The only regret I have in life is giving you birth."

Recalled Sondheim, "As quickly as my hand could cross the paper I wrote her a three-page reply. Everything I'd felt, that I'd never expressed up to this point. It wasn't hard. I just said, 'I don't want to see you any more. I'll continue to support you, and just call my business manager'; that was all."

That catharsis could not heal the childhood wounds. Sondheim wouldn't permit himself to fall in love with anyone. If the relationship didn't work out, the pain would be unbearable; look at what the theater had just done to him. He told people that he was thinking about forsaking composition altogether, that perhaps he'd try to write mystery novels. But this would have been like Canute commanding the tide to reverse itself, and he knew it.

In 1984, Sondheim tentatively edged back into the creative mind-set, working with dramatist James Lapine, making certain to avoid the mainstream in every respect—musically, lyrically, conceptually. He wanted to do something totally different this time—not only from what others might offer but also from anything he had written before. He intended to push and prod the audience, even against its will, to recognize the American musical as an art form as valid as opera or jazz.

And, in fact, when *Sunday in the Park with George* debuted at the Booth Theater in 1985, critics could find no basis of comparison with any other musical, for the show had taken on nothing less than the act of creation. Its subject: the pointillist painter Georges Seurat and his effort to create a fresh way of looking at the physical world. Although *Sunday* had a romantic air, and Tony Straiges's remarkable sets evoked *fin-de-siècle* Paris, even the love songs addressed the compensations and demands of art. The first act focused on the painter as he outlined the painting that established his name, "Sunday Afternoon on the Island of La Grande Jatte." Even the love songs addressed the private rewards of art:

Look, I made a hat—
Where there never was a hat!

The second act audaciously moved within the canvas to show the characters imprisoned forever in George Seurat's work. The third act moved to the twentieth century, to examine Seurat's grandson engaged in a contemporary piece of his own: a motion picture projector.

To give his new work the verbal equivalent of pointillist painting, Sondheim repeated certain small phrases—"color and light," "move on," "bring order to the whole." Musically he used three or four short notes followed by upward-reaching intervals, usually minor thirds or fourths. In the *Times*, John Rockwell delved into the melodic structure: "His use of these little building blocks hardly precludes soaring lyricism, however, especially with the warmly orchestrated sustaining lines to counterpoint the pointillism. At its best, this method recalls the lyrical climaxes in the operas of Leoš Janáček, which are similarly built up from interlocking motifs, repeated over and over in a climactic upward curve."

Reviewers and feature writers tended to be respectful rather than ecstatic, but their enthusiasm picked up considerably when *Sunday* won the Pulitzer Prize—only the sixth musical to win the award. The Pulitzer committee may well have had in mind Frank Rich's shrewd comment in the *Times*: "This protagonist is possibly a double for Mr. Sondheim at his most self-doubting. . . . In keeping with his setting, Mr. Sondheim has written a lovely, wildly inventive score that sometimes remakes the modern French composers whose revolution in music paralleled the post-impressionists' in art."

That *Sunday in the Park with George* failed to earn back its investment counted for nothing; Sondheim's confidence was back, and that was all that mattered to the theatrical community—and to the backers, who had learned to wait for their payoff. A burst of energy followed, along with some competitive sniping at the lyricists who had preceded him. He judged Ira Gershwin "self-conscious." Irving Berlin told jokes very well in his songs, but "I don't think he has ever touched me. I admire him more than I love him." Lorenz Hart had "sloppy" technique and kept writing "the same song over and over again." Some time later, Berlin rose to defend his old colleague: "Stephen Sondheim, a very successful lyric writer, came out of left field with an unkindly, an unjust interview about Larry Hart as a lyric writer. All I can say is that Larry Hart's lyrics have lasted so many years. . . . Larry Hart was not only a lyric writer but a word writer. He had a fine education and could use four- and five- and six- and seven-letter words, and still get down to writing 'With a Song in My Heart.' I mean, he could be very simple. And very moving, when a lot of others can't be."

In mitigation, no one was harder on Sondheim than Sondheim. Weighing some of his work in *West Side Story*, for example, he disparaged the internal rhymes for "I Feel Pretty" ("It's alarming how charming I feel") as too mannered for the uneducated Maria. And he was especially critical of "America":

"I had this wonderful quatrain that went,

Everything free in America,
For a small fee in America.

"The 'For a small fee' was my little zinger—except that the 'for' is accented and 'small fee' is impossible to say that fast, so it went '*For* a smafee in America.' Nobody knew what it meant!"

There would be no such flaws in Sondheim's next production, *Into the Woods*. The musical premiered on Broadway in 1987 and became his second-greatest success. Again working with Lapine, he took inspiration from psychiatrist Bruno Bettelheim's great explication of fairy tales, *The Uses of Enchantment*. To Bettelheim, the woods of the tales have always "symbolized the dark, hidden, near-impenetrable world of our unconscious. . . . When we succeed in finding our way out we shall emerge with a much more highly developed humanity." Accordingly, *Into the Woods* interwove several classic fairy tales, among them Jack and the Beanstalk, Cinderella, and Little Red Riding Hood.

Act 1 narrated the traditional story, but Act 2 was something else again: a twice-upon-a-time narrative, following the principals past the standard "happily ever after" conclusion. Cinderella finds that life in the castle isn't what she imagined; the giant's wife terrorizes a village, furiously pursuing the man who killed her husband; Prince Charming enjoys a liaison with a baker's wife in the forest. Violence ensues before everything rights itself in the finale.

When Sondheim was on his game—particularly in Act 1—he was both hilarious and charming. Confronting Little Red Riding Hood, for example, the Wolf licks his lips and sings of the pleasures of the flesh, by which he means enjoyment in every sense of the word. The vulpine villain recalls two victims, the naive and comely Little Riding Hood. And she was only one highlight of the day. He also derived great satisfaction from her delectable grandmother. It's impossible, he burbles:

To describe what you feel
When you're talking to your meal.

The trouble with the plot—and the score—was its insistence on turning everything on its ear, jeering at tradition in a grotesque and angry way. It seemed a paean to relativism, an insistence on the individual's rights, at whatever cost to the community. One of the songs, "No One Is Alone," became something of an anthem for AIDS sufferers. Unlike most Sondheim numbers, this one supplies a moral, as befits the subject of the show. It addresses those who feel forsaken and solitary. "All fairy tales are parables about steps to maturity," the songwriter told the *New York Times*. "The final step is when you feel connected to the rest of the world." For the book writer, James Lapine, "the second act is very much about the legacy of what our parents teach us and how, even if we've rebelled against them, we hand that down to our children. For me, it isn't just parents and children, but everybody who teaches or is an artist. 'No One Is Alone' is about how we are all interconnected." Thus:

You decide what's good
You decide alone
But no one is alone.

In that statement a larger problem resides. If no one is alone, then an isolated decision is impossible. Yet if an individual does act on his own, then everything—good, evil, sorrow, bliss—is relative, and nothing is permanent.

"No One Is Alone" makes an interesting contrast to a similar number, "You'll Never Walk Alone," written more than half a century earlier by Richard Rodgers and Oscar Hammerstein II.

When you walk through a storm hold your head up high
And don't be afraid of the dark.
At the end of the storm is a golden sky
And the sweet silver song of a lark.
Walk on through the wind,
Walk on through the rain,
Though your dreams be tossed and blown.
Walk on, walk on, with hope in your heart
And you'll never walk alone;
You'll never walk alone.

The difference is one both of sincerity and authenticity. Hammerstein's lyric seems the authentic utterance of a congenital optimist who believes what he says. Sondheim's rings false, the work of someone who doesn't quite stand behind his words. The man who failed to attend his mother's funeral, for example, is hardly in a position to advise others, vis-à-vis parents, to "honor their mistakes." As for the notion that "you decide what's right, you decide what's good"—can the moral relativist who wrote that line be the same man who once showed teenage punks mocking the experts who blamed their gangbanging on their victimization by bad parents and lack of economic opportunity rather than on their own exuberantly free choice?

Nonetheless, on the strength of the sparkling score, Bernadette Peters's star turn as a witch and Joanna Gleason's as the baker's wife, and the popular (and correct) belief that *Into the Woods* was the only kind of "family show" Sondheim would ever write, the production thrived at the box office. It ran for 764 performances, received ten Tony nominations, and in a season overwhelmed by Andrew Lloyd Webber's spectacular *The Phantom of the Opera*, won in the Best Score category. Lapine won another award for Best Book, and Gleason took honors for Best Actress.

The songwriter was to go on, but this would be the best of his last hurrahs. To demonstrate that he could write "singles" as well as a score, he contributed songs to several films, among them *The Seven Percent Solution* and *Dick Tracy*. For the latter movie, a live-action comic strip, he wrote "Sooner or Later" simply because the title roleist, Warren Beatty, asked him to. "I'd done a score for him for *Reds*," recalled Sondheim, "and I'd never quite finished it. . . . Warren was very patient"—but at the time yet another Broadway show was distracting the songwriter—"so I always felt I owed him one."

The debt was amply paid when Madonna, of all people, sang "Sooner." She had made a public fuss about learning a Sondheim song "with all those sharps and flats," but then she went on the sound stage to perform with stylish felicity, making full use of triple rhymes:

> *. . . it's time, so why waste it in chatter?*
> *Let's settle the matter.*
> *Baby, you're mine on a platter.*

"Sooner or Later" won an Academy Award in the category of Best Original Song for 1991, and Madonna gave it some extra spin when she performed it in a lounge setting on her Blonde Ambition tour, and included it on her album *I'm Breathless.*

This was no surprise to Sondheim's ever-increasing fan base. Several years before, he had been engaged to write a number for the Sherlock Holmes film *The Seven Percent Solution.* Here he showed an ability to out-entendre Cole Porter with a song entitled "I Never Do Anything Twice," about a lady of easy virtue and an abbot who wants her to dress in a wimple and veil—to no avail because by then she has developed more catholic tastes.

You've my highest regard, and I know that it's hard.
Still no matter the vice, I never do anything twice.

Over the last ten years or so, almost all of Sondheim's musicals have enjoyed revivals, either on Broadway or the West End (even a forty-minute sketch, *The Frogs,* wound up as a lively two-hour off-Broadway farce). Even so, the composer refused to satisfy himself with the sights in his rearview mirror. For the 1994 musical *Passion,* an adaptation of an obscure Italian film, he again tried something completely new. Weary of operatic, showstopping moments that brought the action to a halt, he crafted his songs to begin and end in dialogue, with no opportunities for applause. To his dismay, it turned out that audiences *wanted* the show to stop after big arias by the lead, Donna Murphy. Denied the opportunity, they grew restive. Word of mouth was extremely negative, and the show closed before the season was out.

Sondheim licked his wounds and pressed on. *Assassins* sought to send up the American "can-do" spirit. Staged like a carnival, it put such presidential killers as John Wilkes Booth and Lee Harvey Oswald up against wannabes like Lynette "Squeaky" Fromme and

Sarah Jane Moore, the two women who tried to slay Gerald Ford. The nineteenth-century assassins exchanged thoughts with their twentieth-century counterparts, with everyone egging everyone else on between songs. The numbers represented Sondheim at his most perverse: vinegary music and a series of cynical internal rhymes.

No job? Cupboard bare?
One room, no one there?
Hey, pal, don't despair;
You wanna shoot a president?

The style was reminiscent of Gore Vidal doing American history in full bitch-revisionist mode (George Washington as a bumbling, pear-shaped soldier, Thomas Jefferson a double-dealing hypocrite, and the like). *Assassins*, workshopped and polished for ten years, did have moments of intensity and some weirdly comic interludes, as when the drugged-out Fromme defends her demented hero Charles Manson: Charley may not be much to look at, but "at least he's the son of God." Unhappily, like so many Sondheim efforts, the show was cold and unlikable. In the end, the theater piece was one more instance of ironic postmodernism separating itself from emotion and paying the box-office price.

When Meryle Secrest's Sondheim biography appeared, it came as no surprise to learn that the composer was sixty-one before he let anyone move in with him. (He lived with the composer Peter Jones for several years, but they broke up.) After all, Sondheim characterized himself as "the boy in the bubble," and he has remained that enclosed child for seventy-plus years. More than once he has said that he "never grew up," and that self-appraisal seems to contain more candor than caricature.

And yet, however high his standards of prosody and musical composition, he has relaxed his standards about the stuff he chooses to ornament. Lately he seems to have *no* standards at all, save those of proper meter and melody, and he has lost himself in a cul-de-sac: what he writes is increasingly bright, superficial, pseudo-perceptive, a glistening maze with no exit. In 2003 a satire called *Musical of Musicals, The Musical*, opened off-Broadway. Its creators, Joanne Bogart and Eric Rockwell, mocked the composer's intricate style:

I'm weary. Be wary of the weary. Don't worry if it's scary.
But wary isn't eerie. Be leery of the wary.
Are you with me? Stay with me.
This is all too deep. I'm falling asleep.
When you have to strain to explain the arcane
It's bound to sound profound.

An unkind portrait of a conflicted genius perhaps, but not inaccurate. Today Sondheim has been working on another musical with John Weidman. *Wise Guys* intends to present the double biographies of two once-famous brothers, Addison and Wilson Mizner, one gay, one straight. In the composer's view, the siblings represent "two divergent aspects of American energy, the builder and the squanderer, the visionary and the promoter, the conformist and the maverick, the idealist planner and the restless cynic, the one who uses things and the one who uses them up." Sondheim remarks that *Wise Guys* is "about to set a record" for gestation. It has been more than fifty years since he first came across their story and started to turn it into a musical. "Bizarre as it may seem, I believe the delay has been good for it."

Only a full-scale production will tell. But even if it never finds a home, people will be arguing about the two Sondheims for generations to come, thanks in large part to the press. The disconnect between the adoring critics and the critical ticket holders began decades ago and has only widened since. Even as the general public turned away, reviewers and academics, sick of the pop pap that has become a large part of Broadway fare, have either celebrated or overlooked the composer's lack of melody and the lyricist's absence of warmth. Something astringent tends to clear their heads. The critics also like to nourish the illusion that they are guiding public taste, leading it to undreamed-of modernist heights. Sondheim has responded by giving them ingenious and elaborate coterie compositions, growing more obscure and off-putting as the years advance.

Yet though the artist has won greater academic honors than Rodgers, Berlin, Hart, the Gershwins, and other front-rank showmen, he has paid a price for his critical renown. Save for a handful of numbers, it is unlikely that fifty years from now popular entertainers will sing his songs and that the general public—those uncelebrated people who finally determine what Broadway and Tin Pan Alley figures enter the pantheon—will cherish them. Such eminence was well within Sondheim's reach, but he didn't take that road. He had better things to do. For better or worse, he still does. At seventy-six, the boy in the bubble can't be bothered with popularity. He's too busy making a hat.

Selected Bibliography

A LITTLE TOUCH OF MOZART IN NEW YORK

Rodney Bolt, *The Librettist of Venice: The Remarkable Life of Lorenzo Da Ponte, Mozart's Poet, Casanova's Friend, and Italian Opera's Impresario in America* (New York: Bloomsbury, 2006).

Memoirs of Lorenzo Da Ponte, translated from the Italian by Elisabeth Abbott (New York: New York Review Books, 2000).

VAUDEVILLE'S BRIEF, SHINING MOMENT

Stefan Kanfer, *Groucho: The Life and Times of Julius Henry Marx* (New York: Alfred A. Knopf, 2000).

Charles and Louise Samuels, *Once Upon a Stage: The Merry World of Vaudeville* (New York, Dodd, Mead, 1974).

Trav S.D., *No Applause—Just Throw Money: The Book That Made Vaudeville Famous* (New York: Faber and Faber, 2005).

Sophie Tucker, *Some of These Days* (Garden City, N.Y.: Doubleday, 1945).

THE AMERICANIZATION OF IRVING BERLIN

Mary Ellin Barrett, *Irving Berlin: A Daughter's Memoir* (New York: Simon & Schuster, 1994).

Laurence Bergreen, *As Thousands Cheer: The Life of Irving Berlin* (New York: Viking, 1990).

Edward Jablonski, *Irving Berlin: American Troubadour* (New York: Henry Holt, 1999).

Robert Kimball and Linda Emmet, eds., *The Complete Lyrics of Irving Berlin* (New York: Alfred A. Knopf, 2000).

THE YIDDISH THEATER'S TRIUMPH

Stefan Kanfer, *Stardust Lost: The Triumph, Tragedy and Mishugas of the Yiddish Theater in America* (New York: Alfred A. Knopf, 2006).

Lulla Rosenfeld, *Bright Star of Exile: Jacob Adler and the Yiddish Theatre* (New York: Thomas Y. Crowell, 1977).

Nahma Sandrow, *Vagabond Stars: A World History of Yiddish Theater* (Syracuse, N.Y.: Syracuse University Press, 1996).

THE DYNAMO AND THE JEWELER

Ira Gershwin, *Lyrics on Several Occasions* (New York: Limelight Editions, 1977).

Edward Jablonski, *George Gershwin* (New York, Putnam, 1962).

Edward Jablonski and Lawrence D. Stewart, *The Gershwin Years: George and Ira* (New York: Da Capo Press, 1996).

Robert Kimball, ed., *The Complete Lyrics of Ira Gershwin* (New York: Alfred A. Knopf, 1993).

THE VOODOO THAT HE DID SO WELL

George Eells, *The Life That Late He Led: A Biography of Cole Porter* (New York: Putnam, 1967).

Robert Kimball, ed., *The Complete Lyrics of Cole Porter* (New York: Alfred A. Knopf, 1983).

Cole Porter, *The Cole Porter Story*, as told to Richard G. Hubler (Cleveland: World Publishing Co., 1965).

RICHARD RODGERS: ENIGMA VARIATIONS

Hugh Fordin, *Getting to Know Him: A Biography of Oscar Hammerstein II* (New York: Random House, 1977).

Dorothy Hart and Robert Kimball, eds., *The Complete Lyrics of Lorenz Hart* (New York: Alfred A. Knopf, 1986).

Frederick Nolan, *Lorenz Hart: A Poet on Broadway* (New York: Oxford University Press, 1994).

Richard Rodgers, *Musical Stages: An Autobiography* (New York: Da Capo Press, 1995).

Meryle Secrest, *Somewhere for Me: A Biography of Richard Rodgers* (New York: Alfred A. Knopf, 2001).

SONDHEIM VS. SONDHEIM

Sandor Goodheart, ed., *Reading Stephen Sondheim: A Collection of Critical Essays* (New York: Garland, 2000).

Meryle Secrest, *Stephen Sondheim: A Life* (New York: Alfred A. Knopf, 1998).

Craig Zadan, *Sondheim & Co.* (New York: Da Capo Press, 1994).

Permissions

The author and the publishers are grateful to the following sources for permission to reprint portions of lyrics in the book.

"Anything Goes." Words and Music by Cole Porter. © 1934 (renewed) WB Music Corp. All rights reserved. Used by permission.

"The Bad in Every Man." Words by Lorenz Hart. Music by Richard Rodgers. © 1934 (renewed) Metro-Goldwyn-Mayer, Inc. All rights controlled by EMI Robbins Catalog, Inc. (Publishing) and Alfred Publishing Co., Inc. (Print). All rights reserved. Used by permission.

"Blue Moon." Lyrics by Lorenz Hart. Music by Richard Rodgers. © 1934 (renewed) Metro-Goldwyn-Mayer, Inc. All rights controlled by EMI Robbins Catalog, Inc. (Publishing) and Alfred Publishing Co., Inc. (Print). All rights reserved. Used by permission.

"Brush Up Your Shakespeare" (from *Kiss Me Kate*). Words and music by Cole Porter. © 1949 (renewed) Chappell & Co. All rights reserved. Used by permission.

"Business Is Business" by Irving Berlin. © Copyright 1911 Ted Snyder Co. © Copyright renewed and assigned to Irving Berlin. International copyright secured. All rights reserved. Used by permission.

"Doin' What Comes Natur'lly" by Irving Berlin. © Copyright 1946 Irving Berlin. © Copyright renewed. International copyright secured. All rights reserved. Used by permission.

"Don't Fence Me In" (from *Hollywood Canteen*). Words and music by Cole Porter. © 1944 (renewed) WB Music Corp. All rights reserved. Used by permission.

"Getting Married Today" from the musical *Company*. Words and music by Stephen Sondheim. Used by permission of Herald Square Music, Inc., on behalf of Range Road Music, Inc., Jerry Leiber Music, Mike Stoller Music, and Rilting Music, Inc.

"Fair Exchange" by Irving Berlin. © Copyright 2001 by The Estate of Irving Berlin. International copyright secured. All rights reserved. Used by permission.

"God Bless America" by Irving Berlin. © Copyright 1938, 1939 by Irving Berlin. © Copyright renewed 1965, 1966 by Irving Berlin. © Copyright assigned the Trustees of the God Bless America Fund. International copyright secured. All rights reserved. Used by permission.

"How Do You Do It, Mabel, on Twenty Dollars a Week?" by Irving Berlin. © Copyright 1911 Ted Snyder Co. © Copyright renewed and assigned to Irving Berlin. International copyright secured. All rights reserved. Used by permission.

"If I Loved You" by Richard Rodgers and Oscar Hammerstein II. Copyright © 1945 by Williamson Music. Copyright renewed. International copyright secured. All rights reserved. Used by permission.

"I Get a Kick Out of You" (from *Anything Goes*). Words and Music by Cole Porter. © 1934 (renewed) WB Music Corp. All rights reserved. Used by permission.

"I Happen to Like New York" (from *The New Yorkers*). Words and music by Cole Porter. © 1931 (renewed) Warner Bros., Inc. All rights reserved. Used by permission.

"I'm Still Here" from the musical *Follies*. Words and music by Stephen Sondheim. Used by permission of Herald Square Music, Inc., on behalf of Range Road Music, Inc., Jerry Leiber Music, Mike Stoller Music, and Rilting Music, Inc.

"The International Rag" by Irving Berlin. © Copyright 1913 by Irving Berlin. © Copyright renewed. International copyright secured. All rights reserved. Used by permission.

"Isn't It Romantic" from the Paramount Picture *Love Me Tonight*. Words by Lorenz Hart. Music by Richard Rodgers. Copyright © 1932 (renewed 1959) by Famous Music LLC. International copyright secured. All rights reserved.

"I Wish I Were in Love Again" by Richard Rodgers and Lorenz Hart. Copyright © 1937 (renewed) Chappel & Co. and Williamson Music. International copyright secured. All rights reserved. Used by permission.

"The Ladies Who Lunch" from the musical *Company*. Words and music by Stephen Sondheim. Used by permission of Herald Square Music, Inc., on behalf of Range Road Music, Inc., Jerry Leiber Music, Mike Stoller Music, and Rilting Music, Inc.

"Let's Do It." Words and Music by Cole Porter. © 1928 (renewed) WB Music Corp. All rights reserved. Used by permission.

"The Little Things You Do Together" from the musical *Company*. Words and music by Stephen Sondheim. Used by permission of Herald Square Music, Inc., on behalf of Range Road Music, Inc., Jerry Leiber Music, Mike Stoller Music, and Rilting Music, Inc.

"Look Out for the Bolsheviki Man" by Irving Berlin. © Copyright 1919 T. B. Harms Co. © Copyright renewed and assigned to Irving Berlin. International copyright secured. All rights reserved. Used by permission.

"Love for Sale." Words and music by Cole Porter. © 1930 (renewed) WB Music Corp. All rights reserved. Used by permission.

"Manhattan." Words and music by Richard Rodgers and Lorenz Hart. Used by permission of Edward B. Marks Music Company.

"Marie from Sunny Italy" by Irving Berlin. © Copyright 1907 Jos. W. Stern & Company. © Copyright renewed and assigned to Irving Berlin. International copyright secured. All rights reserved. Used by permission.

"Mountain Greenery" by Richard Rodgers and Lorenz Hart. © 1926 (renewed) WB Music Corp. and Williamson Music. International copyright secured. All rights reserved. Used by permission.

"My Wife's Gone to the Country (Hurrah! Hurrah!)" by Irving Berlin. © Copyright 1909 Ted Snyder Co. © Copyright renewed and assigned to Irving Berlin. International copyright secured. All rights reserved. Used by permission.

"Night and Day." Words and Music by Cole Porter. © 1932 (renewed) WB Music Corp. All rights reserved. Used by permission.

"Oh! How I Hate to Get Up in the Morning" by Irving Berlin. © Copyright 1918 Waterson, Berlin & Snyder Co. © Copyright renewed and assigned to Irving Berlin. International copyright secured. All rights reserved. Used by permission.

"Please Don't Monkey with Broadway." Words and Music by Cole Porter. © 1940 (renewed) Chappell & Co., Inc. All rights reserved. Used by permission.

"Prayer." Words by Lorenz Hart. Music by Richard Rodgers. Print rights administered by Alfred Publishing Co., Inc. All rights reserved. Used by permission.

"Sadie Salome (Go Home)" by Irving Berlin. Copyright 1909 Ted Snyder Co. © Copyright renewed and assigned to Irving Berlin. International copyright secured. All rights reserved. Used by permission.

"Sorry—Grateful" from the musical *Company*. Words and music by Stephen Sondheim. Used by permission of Herald Square Music, Inc., on behalf of Range Road Music, Inc., Jerry Leiber Music, Mike Stoller Music, and Rilting Music, Inc.

"Supper Time" by Irving Berlin. © Copyright 1933 Irving Berlin, Inc. © Copyright renewed. International copyright secured. All rights reserved. Used by permission.

"The Sweetest Sounds" by Richard Rodgers. © 1962 by Williamson Music. © Copyright renewed. International copyright secured. All rights reserved. Used by permission.

"Ten Cents a Dance" by Richard Rodgers and Lorenz Hart. © 1930 (renewed) WB Music Corp. and Williamson Music. International copyright secured. All rights reserved. Used by permission.

"Thank You So Much Missus Lowsborough—Goodby." Words and music by Cole Porter. © 1934 (renewed) Warner Bros., Inc. All rights reserved. Used by permission.

"That Revolutionary Rag." © Copyright 1919 T. B. Harms Co. © Copyright renewed and assigned to Irving Berlin. International copyright secured. All rights reserved. Used by permission.

"There's No Business Like Show Business" by Irving Berlin. © Copyright 1946 by Irving Berlin. © Copyright renewed. International copyright secured. All rights reserved. Used by permission.

"They Like Ike" by Irving Berlin. © Copyright 1950 Irving Berlin. © Copyright renewed. International copyright secured. All rights reserved. Used by permission.

"To Keep My Love Alive" (from *A Connecticut Yankee*). Words by Lorenz Hart. Music by Richard Rodgers. © 1944 (renewed) Warner Bros. Inc. and Williamson Music, Inc. All rights reserved. Used by permission.

"Top Hat, White Tie and Tails" by Irving Berlin. © Copyright 1935 Irving Berlin. © Copyright renewed. International copyright secured. All rights reserved. Used by permission.

"Weren't We Fools." Words and music by Cole Porter. © 1927 (renewed) WB Music Corp. All rights reserved. Used by permission.

"When I Lost You" by Irving Berlin. © Copyright 1912 Waterson, Berlin & Snyder Co. © Copyright renewed and assigned to Irving Berlin. International copyright secured. All rights reserved. Used by permission.

"You'd Be So Nice to Come Home To." Words and music by Cole Porter. © 1942 (renewed) by Chappell & Co. All rights reserved. Used by permission.

"You Do Something to Me." Words and music by Cole Porter. © 1929 (renewed) Warner Bros., Inc. All rights reserved. Used by permission.

"You'll Never Walk Alone" by Richard Rodgers and Oscar Hammerstein II. Copyright © 1945 by Williamson Music. Copyright renewed. International copyright secured. All rights reserved. Used by permission.

"You're the Top" (from *Anything Goes*). Words and Music by Cole Porter. © 1934 (renewed) Warner Bros., Inc. All rights reserved. Used by permission.

"You're the Top Parody" by Irving Berlin. © Copyright 2001 by The Estate of Irving Berlin. International copyright secured. All rights reserved. Used by permission.

"You Took Advantage of Me" (from *Present Arms*). Words by Lorenz Hart. Music by Richard Rodgers. © 1928 (renewed) Warner Bros., Inc. All rights reserved. Rights for the extended renewal term in the United States controlled by The Estate of Lorenz Hart and Williamson Music. All rights on behalf of The Estate of Lorenz Hart administered by WB Music Corp. All rights reserved. Used by permission.

"You Took Advantage of Me" by Richard Rodgers and Lorenz Hart. © 1928 (renewed) WB Music Corp. and Williamson Music. International copyright secured. All rights reserved. Used by permission.

"You've Got to Be Carefully Taught" by Richard Rodgers and Oscar Hammerstein II. Copyright © 1949 by Richard Rodgers and Oscar Hammerstein II. Copyright renewed Williamson Music, owner of publication and allied rights throughout the world. International copyright secured. All rights reserved. Used by permission.

Index

A NOTE ON THE AUTHOR

Stefan Kanfer's writings and criticism have appeared in most major publications, and his most recent books include *Stardust Lost*, a history of the Yiddish theater; *Ball of Fire*, about the sources of Lucille Ball's comedy; *Groucho*; and *The Last Empire*, a social history of the De Beers diamond company. At *Time* magazine for more than twenty years, he is now a contributing editor of *City Journal* and a Literary Lion of the New York Public Library. He lives in New York and Cape Cod.